Lifetime Sermons

+ Evangelical and Evangelistical +

+ Scriptural and Substantive +

+ Timely and Timeless +

Volume I

E. Dale Click

E. Dale Click

CSS Publishing Co., Inc.
Lima, Ohio

TIMELESS LIFETIME SERMONS

FIRST EDITION
Copyright @ 2011 by
E. Dale Click

All rights reserved. No portion of this book may be reproduced or utilized in any form or by any means, electronic or mechanical including photocopying, without permission in writing from the author. Inquiries should be addressed to: EDC805@aol.com.

Scripture quotations are from the New Revised Standard Version of the Bible, copyright 1989 by the Division of Christian Education of the National Council of the Church of Christ in the USA. Used by permission.

Library of Congress Control Number: 2011920935

ISBN-13: 978-0-7880-2237-1
ISBN-10: 0-7880-2237-7

PRINTED IN USA

Book Reviews

When you ask yourself how to build and strengthen a church there is only one answer -- you preach the Word of God and people will come and continue to do so... you do not put on theatre. I especially like your theology... there is no compromise in your sermons because there is no compromise in the Bible... where can the world find more men like Dale Click?
Noble Trenham
First Global Capital Ventures, CEO
Pasadena, California

My favorite sermon was "A Lesson on Humility." I have often thought about humility. What I had not thought about is what it takes to have humility — gratitude, reverence, and forgiveness. Thanks for putting humility in perspective describing the behaviors it takes to be humble.
Gerry Turner
President 2010-2011
Rotary Club of Los Angeles

Throughout the book Pastor Click's sermons reveal his passion for evangelism through preaching the Word in worship.
Margaret A. Krych
Faculty
The Lutheran Theological Seminary at Philadelphia

Table of Contents

Preface	**7**
Reflections on the Preparation and Proclamation of a Sermon	**21**
Sermon 1 Chief Obstacle of the Church	**31**
Sermon 2 The Circle of Redemption	**36**
Sermon 3 A Hell There Is	**41**
Sermon 4 Lessons at a Lake	**46**
Sermon 5 Parable of the Elder Brother	**52**
Sermon 6 Parable of the Friend at Midnight	**57**
Sermon 7 Parable of the Rich Farmer	**62**
Sermon 8 Parable of the Two Builders	**67**
Sermon 9 Parable of the House that Was Swept Clean and Left Empty	**71**
Sermon 10 Parable of the Last Judgment	**76**
Sermon 11 Christ at the Bier	**81**
Sermon 12 A Lesson on Humility	**86**
Sermon 13 Take Heart — Sin Forgiven!	**90**
Sermon 14 Parable of the Marriage Feast	**92**
Sermon 15 Saint Luke, an Evangelist	**95**
Sermon 16 Luther's Love Life	**99**
Sermon 17 Honoring the Saints	**105**
Sermon 18 To Whom Much Is Given	**110**
Sermon 19 Confession for Young and Older	**115**
Sermon 20 Jeremiah and the New Covenant	**119**
Sermon 21 With One Voice	**123**
Sermon 22 Prepare the Way	**127**
Sermon 23 What Christ Is Like — A Shepherd	**132**
Sermon 24 What Christ Is Like — An Angel	**137**
Sermon 25 What Christ Is Like — A Master	**143**

Preface

For years I resisted the temptation to publish my sermons. Why? Not because of humility because I am not known for that cherished characteristic! Because I am unknown except in a few small circles. Who would read them?

One day I walked into a Best Buy store shopping for a scanner. A young clerk asked me, "What do you want to do with a scanner?" I replied, "I want to scan sermons." The clerk replied, "What's a sermon?"

Appalled by the young man's lack of religious knowledge, I asked, "Where do you attend church?" An evangelism specialist, this is a question I teach people to inquire wherever they go, always assuming people questioned attend church! If they worship, I exchange ideas with them. If they don't attend church, I invite them to worship at my church, offering them lunch after worship. This often results in people attending church with me! I pay for the luncheon from my tithe! I learned from business people their practice of treating people to lunch or dinner to discuss business. Why not for Christian business?!

The young clerk replied, "I don't go to church and never have." He repeated the question, "What's a sermon?" I explained and invited him to worship. I never bought a scanner that day. And, the young man didn't attend church with me. I never worry about the results of my invitations; I realize, however, my responsibility, as a Christian, to plant seeds. Later I returned to the store and gave the young clerk one of my sermons!

This young man epitomizes our culture. I felt like preaching a sermon to him right then and there, but I restrained myself! I thanked the Lord I had written a sermon titled "What It Means To Believe" and the copy I gave the Best Buy clerk was to teach him not only what a sermon is but what a sermon does.

Age is another reason I have hesitated to have my sermons published. When I was young I thought no one would read my sermons. When I became older, I succumbed to realize that few listen to older people. Prompted by the Best Buy episode, I concluded that age didn't really matter. If you have something worthwhile to say, say it! I am saying it in this first volume of sermons.

I could sum up my life in a paragraph, or in several sentences. Since I am writing on a preacher's subject, I have decided to share some life experiences so that you can picture a preacher in the making.

I was born on a farm in Clark County, Ohio, on a late Thursday, August 29, 1918. (Yes, I know darling, I am growing old...). They say my mother stood on her head in bed to prevent my birth until the doctor arrived! Friends say that explains who I am!

My first experience with death was when my dog, Buddy, was killed. He always met me when I came from school on the corner near our house on Pleasant Street in Springfield, Ohio. One day he didn't meet me. He had been run over by a truck. At the age of seven I sobbed into the night. I discovered that death is mysterious.

My first remembered experience of life was when I was four years old. I was in the kitchen on the farm. It was dark. I told Mother I wanted to go out to the barn and watch Dad milk the cows. She said, "You can't do that! It is dark outside." I replied, "I can see Dad's lantern in the barn and I will keep my eye on it. May I go?" My mother must have watched me from a distance! When I was halfway to the barn I became scared because an owl began to hoot. But, I kept going and kept my eye on Dad's lantern and arrived safely. Dad was surprised to see me. He picked me up in his arms and hugged me! That's the only time I remember my dad doing that. He was not very expressive that way. But, I learned a lesson from that experience: always keep your eye on your Heavenly Father's lantern and you will reach His intended destination.

Shortly thereafter, we moved into town (Springfield, Ohio) and lived at Pleasant Street for ten years. I entered school and flunked the first grade. That's pretty hard to do! My parents were dumbfounded. They finally learned I had difficulty hearing and placed me on the front row in the classroom so that I could hear the teacher. But this experience gave me the impression that I was dumb. I carried that thought with me for years and at times still do. Yet, I won a school math contest and first prize for a painting among Springfield elementary students. I dreamed of becoming an artist like my cousin, Richard. If I had become an artist, I would have starved to death! That Indian painting is still hanging in my television room!

During the Depression years I knocked on most household doors in Springfield selling all sorts of items from eggs to hand irons. Every dime counted in those Depression days. I learned how to be a salesman at an early age. It has helped me in ministry since we are all sales people for the Lord. I keep reminding myself that I am only in sales and not in management!

At age fourteen we moved back to a farm. I learned to harness and drive horses, plough, rake hay, and haul manure. I learned to milk cows and slop hogs. I raised a pig for a 4-H Club project and won first prize at the Springfield Fair for my pig called "Honey." I milked cows and slopped the hogs every morning before catching the school bus for Lawrenceville High. I was a star on the high school basketball team, played baseball, and pitched a no hitter in a softball game. Dick Fisher (now deceased) and I won the Clark County doubles tennis tournament. I also won the District championship in typing, typing eighty words a minute but flunked in the State championship. I was president of my high school class in junior and senior years.

I had to take remedial English when I enrolled at Wittenberg University at Springfield, Ohio. This also contributed to my feeling inferior. I didn't graduate with any honors but I did earn a bachelor degree with a major in history.

I attended seminary on the same Wittenberg campus in Springfield. It was known as Hamma Divinity School. I didn't win any honors there, either, but I earned a master of divinity degree.

What influenced me to attend seminary and become a pastor? In the ninth grade I was in North Carolina on vacation with my pastor and his family. We hiked to a revival meeting in the mountains. At the conclusion of worship the traveling evangelist invited people to come forward and accept Jesus Christ as their Savior. I didn't feel like doing that because I was already a believer. But, something entered my mind, as if the Lord were talking to me. The voice said, "There is a young man four rows in back of you. I want you to take him down the aisle to be saved." I said I would if they sang one more stanza of the hymn they were singing, "Shall We Gather at the River." They sang seven more stanzas before I got up enough nerve to approach the young man! How did I know which young man? I don't know. I seemed to know there was a young man who needed Jesus. The young man accompanied me down the aisle and accepted Jesus as his Savior.

I can't explain this at all. It just happened. Ever since that time I felt called to become a pastor. You don't have to have a similar experience to become a pastor; yet, I believe every pastoral candidate needs to feel the Call to serve in a special way, as if God is directing the decision. I felt God put his hand on me that night at a revival. In all my almost seventy years of ministry, I have never swerved from feeling that God led me to become a pastor. I have always felt God sent. That's a great feeling!

I also felt called to serve as a missionary. Perhaps I felt that way because my pastor and his wife, The Rev. Dr. and Mrs. Louis G. Gray, had been missionaries to Japan and the Virgin Islands. I wanted to go to Africa. Upon graduation from seminary I was called to be a missionary to Tanganyika (now Tanzania). Because of World War II I couldn't get passage to travel to Africa. Instead, I was called to a newly born congregation in California.

While in the last years of college I fell in love with my pastor's daughter, Martha Jane, whose nickname was Bunny. Her parents wanted her to become a missionary. She was five years younger than me. She graduated from high school at the age of fifteen with the highest scholastic honors, won state contests in Latin, English, and History, and was rated superior in piano and voice. She lived in Newberry, South Carolina, with her Aunt Sadie, while in high school because her parents felt she would receive a better education there. When she came back to Springfield, following high school graduation, she entered Business College and acquired skills that would help her through college. We fell in love during this time. We were engaged five years and never had sex until we were married, although we came close a couple times! She went to Agnes Scott College in Decatur, Georgia, a noted Presbyterian college for women, graduated Magna Cum Laude and was elected to Phi Beta Kappa. Her major was the Bible. I was smart enough to marry a smart woman!

We were married June 11, 1944, after my graduation from seminary and ordination and her graduation from college. The president of the California Lutheran Synod, Dr. James P. Beasom, had visited our seminary and offered me the opportunity of becoming pastor of a three-month-old parish, Saint Andrew's Lutheran Church, San Mateo, California. Neither Bunny nor I had been west of Chicago. It took courage to leave families and start marriage and a ministry in new territory. Since we couldn't go to Africa, we went to California!

We served Saint Andrew's nine years. Our two sons, Barry and Dean, were born during that time in San Mateo. With the help of a professional fund-raiser, Guy Lamphear, the congregation was able to purchase a lot on a main thoroughfare and built its first unit. The congregation grew from 28 to over 400 before we left. That parish is still strong!

By accident I sat beside Dr. Franklin C. Koch, Secretary for Social Missions (including evangelism) of the ULCA, at a United Lutheran Church in America convention in Seattle. Somehow he had heard of the growth of Saint Andrew's. He invited me to consider going to New York City, headquarters of the United Lutheran Church in America, and become an Associate Director of Evangelism. In my thirties, I became the youngest executive in the ULCA. My mother's classic statement was, "I never thought you would get so far!"

I discovered something about myself in New York. I not only could teach pastors and lay people the subject of evangelism but I could write. I helped the ULCA decide on a two-year evangelism emphasis (1955-57) which became known as the Lutheran Evangelism Mission. I wrote manuals for regional and congregational committees, describing how to accomplish this church-wide emphasis on evangelism. They labeled me the "architect" of that church-wide program. This was quite a surprise. I traveled throughout the United States, Canada, Puerto Rico, the Virgin Islands, and eventually was sent to Argentina to direct evangelism missions throughout that country. This had never been done and to my knowledge has not been done since. I was so young I never was fearful or gave a second thought to traveling throughout a strange country and directing evangelism missions. I just felt God led!

After that experience, I went back into the parish. In hindsight, I could have stayed at New York and continued being an executive.

11

I was too naive to tell them that was what I wanted to do. When they interviewed me to become Director of Evangelism all I could say was, "Whatever the Lord wants me to do." All they wanted me to say was that I wanted to become the Director of Evangelism. I never did. I thought I was being humble. Maybe that was God's way of returning me to the front line of parish work. President Franklin Clark Fry had always told me not to stay in executive work too long. He said the parish is where the real work of the Lord is accomplished. He always regretted not having the opportunity to return to a parish.

After the New York evangelism experience, I was called to First Lutheran Church of Los Angeles, California, where I served eleven years. I developed preaching skills during that time. I adopted habits of study (spending one day a week in research) and wrote sermon manuscripts that enriched my preaching life. I practiced reading at least a book a week. This central city parish needed a preacher evangelist. I seemed to fit in. We made drastic changes to the property to insure the future of this church, providing parking, a new school building, refurbishing the nave, and installing a magnificent organ. The congregation reached its zenith while I was there. I just happened to be in the right place at the right time. I was led from New York to Los Angeles for a purpose and I knew it. God had overruled my personal executive desires.

Alas, in May 2006, this parish closed. The closing of First Church was like the death of a child to me. The closing service was like a funeral. I witnessed the bishop handing the cross from the altar to a member of the congregation to take out of the church. Tears streamed down my cheeks. I still think it didn't need to happen. I think it was a synod's blunder and a blemish upon the whole church. We are not commissioned to take crosses from altars but to take crosses into surrounding neighborhoods.

From First Church, Los Angeles, I went to Luther Memorial Church in Erie, Pennsylvania, one of our largest Lutheran churches at the time. I think pride influenced me to accept this Call. It resulted in being my "mulligan," if you know anything about golf. Shortly after I arrived we made plans to Call two young pastors who were graduating from Chicago Lutheran Theological Seminary to join me in ministry. Everyone seemed excited at the prospect. After the two young men visited us, we didn't think it necessary to have them return for the special congregational meeting. Over 800 members voted. The decision to Call them lost by seven votes. I knew my ministry was finished at Luther Memorial before it even began. President Robert Marshall of the Lutheran Church in America, a college classmate, told me I was wrong to think that way and that I should stay. I didn't. I didn't feel called to serve a church that seemed to want only a chaplain.

Rotary friends in Los Angeles invited and arranged for me to become Assistant to the Chancellor of Pepperdine University. After serving Pepperdine for over a year, helping them to transfer the campus from downtown Los Angeles to Malibu, I sensed I was in the wrong place and needed to return to a parish. The synod president gave me no opportunity. I felt unwanted, a failure. I needed a job. I needed income. Another Rotary friend, president of Coca-Cola Bottling Company and Arrowhead Puritas Waters in Los Angeles, wanted me in his organization but said at the time he only had an opening with Arrowhead selling water. I accepted. I was running out of money. I drove a large truck, carried big bottles on my shoulder, set up water coolers in homes, and knocked on doors throughout the San Fernando Valley selling water. One day I happened to knock on the door of one of our pastors. The pastor said, "Dale, what are you doing in that uniform?" I replied, "Selling water so that my family can have food on the table." It was a humbling experience. It reminded me of my boyhood days selling eggs from house to house in Springfield, Ohio. I sold water for over a year and became the top salesman. They even took my picture and wrote about my experience in a nation-wide magazine, "Preacher Can Sell Water!" I learned that adversity can not only be endured but you can learn about another dimension of life.

About this time a former colleague in evangelism (Clifton Weihe) was serving a parish in Santa Maria, California, and invited me to supply on occasion. At the same time a parish in Fresno was without a pastor and needed an interim and somebody submitted my name. I was told by the synod president I could go there but I could not become their pastor. I served Good Shepherd, Fresno, several months, commuting from our home in Westlake (a suburb

13

of Los Angeles) to Fresno, 200 miles each way! The congregation became convinced I should become their pastor and told the synod they wanted me as pastor. Two physicians spearheaded the movement. This was not of my doing. It just happened. The synod president was not happy about this and berated me. Chagrined, he pointed out that I would be making more money than most pastors in synod! I served there five years.

The church kept growing while I was at Good Shepherd. One of the physicians who had been instrumental in having me become their pastor was more an influence than I realized. Evidently through the years members looked to him instead of their pastor for direction. He was a good man and had good intentions. To my surprise, he opposed me when I stood firm on the evangelism thrust of the congregation. I didn't see it coming. He formed a group of fifty people and invited the synod to send a committee for an open hearing about my ministry. It was like a trial. I didn't say a word. It was painful to hear people openly condemn me. My wife was crushed. A lay person on the synod committee thought I should resign. I did not. The physician and his fifty people left the congregation and went elsewhere. Nevertheless, Good Shepherd regained its strength in a relatively short time.

Dr. Roland Bainton, world authority on Luther and Yale professor (now deceased), became a friend and lectured at Good Shepherd on the teachings and times of Luther. He stayed in our home while teaching at Good Shepherd. He told me one evening what his father had told him, "Unless you have been kicked out of at least one church, you haven't been much of a preacher!" He learned what had transpired at Good Shepherd. I was almost kicked out! I am happy to report that parish continues to thrive and has relocated.

I probably would have stayed longer at Good Shepherd if it had not been for an unexpected telephone call from the east. Dr. Kenneth Sauer, Bishop of the Ohio Synod, who was a young man when I was going around the country as an evangelism director and was influenced by the Lutheran Evangelism Mission, telephoned me about one of his downtown parishes that needed special help. Sauer knew about my ministry not only in evangelism but in central city parishes. He also knew my aging parents still lived on a farm

25 miles away from this parish, First Lutheran Church of Dayton, Ohio. He put two and two together and stated I needed to consider moving to Dayton. I was very much a Californian! I wasn't keen on returning to snowy territory. But God does direct lives and I returned to Ohio, my birthplace. My good wife throughout our ministry never once opposed a Call. She wasn't happy to go east, but we did.

At First Church, Dayton, I became convinced a Lutheran Bible study was needed that would give people a handle on the Bible. In Fresno, I heard that some Good Shepherd members were going to a Bible study at the Baptist church. I wondered why. The Associate Pastor, Alan B. Stringfellow, now nationally known in his church for Bible study, taught the class. I marched over there one time to hear his Bible study. Members of Good Shepherd were shocked to see me! So, was Stringfellow!

Stringfellow had a good idea and I realized why Good Shepherd members attended his Bible study. He required everyone attending to read an assigned book of the Bible the week prior. During class time he would review that book and in an hour gave people an understanding of each book of the Bible.

I was convinced we ought to do something similar in the Lutheran church. I tried to entice my wife to create and teach such a study since she was a Phi Beta Kappa and had majored in Bible at college. "Maybe some day," she said.

I pressured her to do such a Bible study at First Church, Dayton. We needed to turn this church around from its downward spiral. At first Bunny declined. She consented to do it after a couple months of husband and wife conversation. Her study would be entirely different from Stringfellow since he was a literalist. But his format was useable anywhere.

We publicized extensively this course of study. We decided to begin it in the summer when many churches have less activity. People kept saying, "You can't do that in the summer. It won't work." But, it worked.

One hundred twenty-five people showed up for the first class session held on a Sunday morning prior to worship! Bunny taught this course and people attended regularly for a year. People became biblically knowledgeable of the entire Bible. I am convinced this study, more than anything else, energized that church. She continued that study for several years and extended it to include various biblical characters.

Tapes were made of Bunny's class sessions. If a person missed a Sunday session they could make up by hearing a tape. Everybody read the Good News Bible. Bunny spent at least twenty hours each week preparing a lesson. Her scholarship, her humor, and her capacity to teach winsomely was a great blessing in our ministry at First Church, Dayton, Ohio.

Bunny died unexpectedly August 31, 1996. I was devastated. She contracted Pancreatic cancer and died within six weeks. I must have said a lot of dumb things in preparing for her death. I thought I knew a lot about death by this time, having pastored hundreds of people through the valley, I discovered I didn't know much at all. I didn't learn about death until an hour after her death as she lay on our bed at home. A smile came across her face. I understood. She had crossed over Jordan.

Son, Barry, transcribed her Bible study tapes. I spent five years editing them and preparing them for publication. These seven volumes titled *Through the Bible — Book by Book* by Martha Jane Gray Click with E. Dale Click, contain meaningful lessons. They should be in church libraries and in homes of Christians. Parishes who teach these lessons will give parishioners a comprehensive understanding of the Bible.

We left First Lutheran Church of Dayton after five years (September 1983). After turning 65, I thought it was the natural thing to do. I was wrong. I discovered I was not content playing golf every day! Since retirement I have written thirteen books (including Bunny's volumes) and I am writing another right now titled *Our Endangered Faith and What Might Be Done about It*. I feel the Christian church as a whole does not realize what is happening, as the young clerk in Best Buy didn't know what a sermon was.

I have served as interim pastor, guest preacher, lecturer on evangelism throughout the country and occasionally abroad, wrote a number of books, and serve as a cruise chaplain twice a year (25 years now) on cruise lines, since my retirement. I established an endowment at Trinity Lutheran Seminary, Columbus, Ohio, titled

The Lutheran Evangelism Mission, to teach pastors the subject of evangelism. Proceeds from the sale of my books are given to this endowment.

On my eightieth birthday I went around the world alone. I finally reached Africa and preached at a church in Tanzania, and went to Japan, including Kumumoto, where Bunny was born, and preached in her church, through the courtesy of Missionary Andrew Ellis, who happened to be sponsored by First Lutheran Church of Dayton, Ohio. Coincidentally, Bunny's father, The Rev. Dr. Louis G. Gray, was also sponsored by First Church.

Now, in my last days, I am preparing these "timeless lifetime sermons" volumes for publication. I feel a sermon worth its salt is timeless. Truth never changes, only references change. How did I choose sermons to be included in this first volume? I didn't. They are chronological beginning with sermons written and preached in the year 1959. I doubt if I will ever see published 23 more years of manuscripts stacked away in my study, even if there is some interest expressed in this first volume!

If you are tempted to think sermons in this volume might be outdated, remember truth never changes; references do. On occasion, I still preach some of these sermons and find congregations as responsive to them as when I first preached them. Seldom do I change the content of a sermon although I might add a quote from a recent book read or relate an appropriate experience. I am convinced a sermon worth its salt needs repeating! This encourages me to offer this first volume.

Lastly, I want to pay tribute to a few people who have influenced, nourished, and contributed to my life. Some are deceased. You can skip these paragraphs, if you wish. I record them because I owe them my gratitude and want to remember them, although I know I have not listed them all. I suggest you may want to make a list also. It is good for the soul!

People who have influenced my life begin with grandparents and parents. I wish I had become as good a parent like them. My parents, especially, were steady and dependable. My wife of 52 years before her death in 1996, not only loved me but was a constant guide and helper. She was the guiding light for our two sons, Barry and Dean, sons who are God's gift to us, and who are now engulfed in making a living in these erratic economic times. My sister, Pauline (now deceased), was smarter and always supportive, as well as her son, retired pastor, Larry Matthews and family. Many cousins come to mind too numerous to list.

Beyond family, I think of an elementary school teacher, Miss Bickle; a junior high teacher, Miss Day; a high school teacher, Miss Hilt; a college professor, Dr. Paul Heisey; seminary professors, Drs. T.A. Kantonen and Elmer Ellsworth Flack; church leaders — United Lutheran Church in America President Franklyn Clark Fry and Secretary Eppling F. Reinartz, and Harold Haas, Director of Social Missions of the ULCA; Dr. James P. Beasom, president of the California Synod, ULCA; colleagues and mentors in ministry, Drs. Wallace E. Fisher and Robert Stackel; college buddy, Ed Goddard; high school buddy, Lester Rust; seminary classmates Ellis Kretschmer and Eldon (Bill) Miller.

I remember parishoners such as Robert and Kitty Arnholt, Carl Cohenour, Marie Gibson, Andy and Edith Forrester, Henry and Edith Fuller, Dan Jacobsen, Carl and Florence Ludvigsen, Ruby Quarfoot and husband, Gordon and Beatrice Ridgeway, Henry Schneider, Marie Soule, Ray and Ev Strack, Stan and Frieda Voll (members of Saint Andrew's, San Mateo, California); Lorraine Bowles, Philip and Becky Conkle, Vi Ewing, Sally Farmer, Robert Fox, Henrietta and Stephanie Gueble, Bill and Barbara Jones, Bud and Ethel Glazebrook, Don Hanson, Don and Steffie Hax, Hildegarde Herfuth, Wayne and Peg Huey, Donald and Stephanie Klempnauer, Dan and Peg Kulp, Dorothy Petersen, Bruce Riley, Richard and Pam Runkle, Jerry and Lois Scott, Ricky Scheiermann, Donald Snyder, Reed and Jean Van Wagenen, Dennis and Karen Whelan, George Wieman (members of First Church, Los Angeles, California); Robert and Helen Collins (members of Luther Memorial, Erie, Pennsylvania); Sandra Borders, Dennis and Penny Fey, John and Lorraine Gear, Ken and Lois Green, John and Pat Gunsett, Robert and Gretchen Jennings, Alma Johnson, Newell and Barbara Johnson, George and Betty Williams, Sam and Carol Umbenhaauer, Neil and Verna Walden (members of Good Shepherd, Fresno, California); Louise Bauman, Billy Doody, Robert and Margaret Gessaman, Lloyd and Ruth Grodrian, the Harshbarger sisters (Katherine, Janet, Martha),

Reuben and Rosalie Hoffman, Robert and Martha Johnson, Grace Rust, Emma Zimmer (members at First Church, Dayton, Ohio); and others this old mind does not presently recall!

I also note Rotary friends: Bob Aldridge, Woody Anderson, Warren Biggs, David Bland, Bogy Bogardus, Don Crocker, Rod Dedeaux, Russ Frandsen, Noel Hatch, Earl Haberlin, Lee Jackman, Joe Kaplan, Marc and Pearl Leeka, Janet Lindstrom, Ken Martinet, Ed and Mary Matveld, Stan Moe, James Pierce, Don Robinson, Ken Rogers, Jim and Carmeletta Simonds, Tom Sullivan, Noble Trenham, Ben Tunnell, Gerry and Kathy Turner, and Steinar Tweiten, to name a few.

+

It is my hope this little story of my life and the chapter following, "Reflections on the Preparation and Proclamation of a Sermon," might whet your appetite to read these sermons. I love the ministry. I love preaching. I hope to keep preaching until the very day I die. Cheers!

E. Dale Click

Reflections on the Preparation and Proclamation of a Sermon

My Mother, Maude, was a Baptist before she married my Lutheran father, Raymond. Consequently, we went to the Lutheran church Sunday mornings and the Baptist church Sunday evenings. She was immersed at her baptism. She told me, "Dale, there is nothing like it!" Although the Lutheran church believes in immersion as well, I was baptized by sprinkling. When I became a Lutheran pastor I had an occasion to baptize people in a river. Mother was right. People felt clean all over!

In my childhood I heard many itinerant preachers, especially in the summertime when there were "Camp Meetings," sometimes in a tent at a campground. I heard Billy Sunday. He literally scared the devil out of me!

I met Billy Graham while in the evangelism department of my church body (The United Lutheran Church in America), in New York City. In talking with Billy and his associates, I asked Billy, "Why don't you go on salary so that people can't accuse you of putting your hand in the till, as some itinerant preachers have done?" He thought it was a good idea. He did that. I can't take credit for it but I may have triggered the thought.

Preaching is second nature for me. Even in high school I was preaching to people in "old folks" homes. In college I did the same thing. In seminary I was sent out, as all students, to preach. I remember preaching in a church somewhere in Kentucky back in the mountains. Somebody had to pump the organ. The young man pumping the organ became so engrossed in my demeanor that he forgot to pump and there was no music!

I have been privileged to preach throughout America, Canada, Puerto Rico, the Virgin Islands, Argentina, Africa, and Japan. They told me I was the first Protestant to preach on radio in Argentina; not too long, however, because Roman Catholics stopped me. I preached outdoors on the campus of the University in Buenos Aires. Roman Catholic students threw stones at me. Stones really hurt, as Stephen in the New Testament documented. I experienced, last year in a visit to South America, things are different now. Roman Catholics and Protestants respect one another.

Lest you feel I might be prejudiced because of the stoning incident, permit me to record another incident. On a weekday morning when I headed to church headquarters in New York City at 231 Madison Avenue, Bishop Fulton Sheen and I would pass one another, stop and chat. We both wore Homberg hats and clerical collars! One time prior to Ash Wednesday, I asked Bishop Sheen what he thought about Lent. "Dale," he said, "we have to climb three flights of stairs for lunch and during Lent it is hardly worth the effort!" There have been many great Roman Catholic preachers. He was one of them. The recent Pope John Paul II was a great preacher.

Dr. Franklin Clark Fry, President of the United Lutheran Church in America, was the preeminent Lutheran preacher in our church while I was in the evangelism department in New York City. Once I met him at the San Francisco airport, took him to dinner, and on to the Episcopal Cathedral where he preached at a Reformation Service. Afterward, he asked me, "Dale, how long did I preach?" I replied, "One hour and thirty seconds!" He said, "Really? I had no idea I preached so long." I said, "Neither did anybody else. It was so interesting!"

Sermons today are often judged by their length instead of by their content. Ten minute sermons are often considered the norm. "Keep it short, preacher!" Attention span is brief these days, unless it is a sports event. How would you like to go to a football game that took only ten minutes?! You would feel cheated that you didn't get your money's worth! Furthermore, too often the substance of short sermons are as brief as their length.

I never heard Martin Luther preach! But, I have read most of his sermons. He didn't mince words. He preached salvation.

I met Martin Luther King in 1952. Both of us were giving lectures at Greenlake, Wisconsin, a Baptist Retreat Center. I spoke on evangelism to Lutherans and he spoke on social issues to Baptists. We spent part of an afternoon together. I asked him, "With a name like yours, why aren't you Lutheran?" He replied,

"Where I come from there are not many Lutheran churches!" He struck me as a sincere person. He didn't just dream.

I don't hear many sermons these days on the subject of "salvation." Preachers like to please people, and the word "salvation" isn't popular. I suspect inviting people to make a decision for Christ is unpopular. People are more interested in getting along in life. Thus, many a preacher has reduced preaching to psychology. Some say if you think "positively" you will get along in this world. Sermon subjects tend to be about people instead of about God and who Christ is.

I once talked with Robert Schuler prior to a Rotary meeting in Los Angeles. I told him I had an idea for him. He replied, "I have plenty of ideas." I said, "I am sure you have for you are known as an idea man. My suggestion is this: Preach a series of sermons on The Life of Christ. People in America don't know who Jesus is. You have access to millions of people and they need to know Jesus." He replied it was a good idea but I never heard him give such a series.

Sermons today don't confront people with decision making. Many preachers go fishing with all line and no hook! Many people leave church without being changed. John the Baptist didn't preach that way. Neither did Jesus!

People today don't seem to like the word "sermon." Bulletins list the sermon as "message." I hesitated to call these volumes *Timeless Lifetime Sermons*. I originally chose the title "Scriptural Descriptions." Still, Webster's definition is correct, "a sermon is a religious discourse by a clergyman as part of a worship service." I hardly think calling Jesus' Sermon on the Mount "Message on the Mount" would have much impact, although the alliteration is attractive!

What does the preacher do before mounting a pulpit and standing before a group of people charged with the responsibility of bringing a word from the Lord? It is an awesome responsibility.

The preacher allocates time for preparation.

It takes a lifetime to prepare a sermon. All the keenness and depth of perception of human life is needed. The capacity to put knowledge and experience into meaningful expressions is needed.

Unwavering belief is needed. Unswerving conviction is needed. Trust in a loving God who always supplies is needed. I am always amazed by how God employs the human mind, especially my own.

I discovered it took me an average of twenty hours to prepare a proper manuscript. I spent another forty hours pastoring. A sixty hour week for me was normal. Maybe I was slow but I simply state what was required in the measure of time to produce sermons and serve the Lord. Count twenty hours times the number of sermons in this volume alone and you realize what it takes to speak on behalf of the Lord. I don't know of any shortcuts.

The preacher reads.

With a background of education including study of the Bible in the original languages of Greek and Hebrew, the preacher has access to information that nurtures the mind. The preacher has a computer at his fingertips making it far easier to write than Saint Paul ever imagined.

The preacher reads the Bible daily. It is also a good idea for the preacher to read, at least, one book a week. Otherwise, there is always the danger of having nothing to say and saying it! I always try to read a book a week.

Sermon preparation for me meant spending Tuesdays in research. Nobody could reach me on a Tuesday unless it was an emergency. Weekday mornings I spent writing about what I had learned from research. By Friday noon I finished the manuscript and the secretary typed it that afternoon while I made hospital calls. On Saturday evening I practiced preaching the sermon and prayed for the gift of the Holy Spirit.

The preacher listens.

The responsible preacher doesn't talk all the time! The preacher listens. The preacher is sensitive to the needs of people and consequently listens to humankind hurts. The preacher is not so much a solver of problems as a salver of human predicaments. The preacher does not pretend to have all answers but claims answers that make life purposeful and meaningful.

It is sometimes difficult to keep silent when tempted to interrupt the flow of conversation. People often are not as much interested in preacher's thoughts as in expressing their own thoughts. People need to get out of them what is on the inside of them. A good listener is not an interrupter. The preacher needs to listen long enough to be able to decipher what is involved.

The preacher not only listens to the hurts of humankind but rejoices in human triumphs! Good things happen to people and as in the Bible, they sing! I always wished for a DVD of Jesus and the disciples singing!

It takes a listener to learn what and how to proclaim what is necessary. Preaching is proclaiming what is necessary and essential. We are not filling up time; we are filling human hearts with eternal truths.

The preacher seeks to understand human nature.

Who does the preacher see standing in a pulpit? Believers, some hot and some cold in the faith: perhaps an unbeliever who has come to worship for the first time and wonders if the preacher is sincere; perhaps a wavering believer who has trouble listening to anybody; or perhaps a sprinkling of believers hungry for a word from the Lord.

I always liked the Greek explanation of the word "sincerity." Their craftsmen made pottery. Some were not too good at it. Poor craftsmens' pottery left holes on the exterior surface. Such craftsmen would fill the holes with wax and then paint over them. Such pottery looked the same as others. A purchaser of poor craftsmanship, however, would soon discover the quality of pottery purchased — in time the wax peeled out. "Sincerity" is without wax. A real preacher is one without wax. A sermon that changes the direction of people is without wax.

The preacher talks with God.

Jesus departed from the disciples at times to be alone and pray. His disciples wondered what happened to him. Much happened; He was filled with the Spirit!

I like to hear a preacher pray during worship. There are church bulletins today with "canned" prayers. The congregation responds to a prayer list with the tiresome words, "Lord, hear our prayer." I often wonder if God pays much attention to automated prayers. I like to hear the preacher pray from the heart and mind. I expect the preacher to have spent several hours in preparing a prayer, after talking with God.

I heard Harry Emerson Fosdick pray at his Riverside Church in New York City. His preaching was eloquent, and from a manuscript! I don't care if the preacher uses a manuscript or notes or an outline. I have tried them all. For years I gave sermons from memory. People were impressed. "He didn't have a single note in front of him," some exclaimed. But, after a decade of that style, I turned to a manuscript. I discovered I needed to say exactly what was intended to be said without letting the emotion of the moment overrule. People who hear me preach know I have something to say. I have always said a sermon is never finished until it is preached and then it is too late!

What impressed me particularly about Fosdick was his prayers. He wrote a book of prayers titled *A Book of Public Prayers*. It is a gem. I wish more pastors wrote prayers as well as sermons.

The preacher tunes his voice.

A Rotary friend and noted preacher, the Rev. Dr. Lloyd Ogilvie, has a great voice. His televised sermons from Hollywood Presbyterian Church reached millions. He became Chaplain of the Senate in Washington, DC. One senator told me, "When Lloyd prays, it is like hearing God speak."

While senior pastor at First Lutheran Church of Los Angeles (11 years), a business man said he thought I should take voice lessons and that he would pay the cost. I found an elderly lady in Hollywood who tuned the human voice. James Mason, the actor, often preceded or followed me for a lesson. I asked him, "You have such a great voice. Why do you take these lessons?" He replied, "The voice needs constant tuning, like an engine. I wish my rector would take lessons, as you are. He has a timid voice. While he may have something worthwhile to say, his message doesn't register. People tune him out."

This elderly teacher would sit at the piano, pound keys, and expect me to imitate the sound. She made me drink water and then she would say "Spit, Reverend Click, spit!" She made me put Vaseline up my nose just before retiring at night. My late wife, Bunny, didn't like that!

Not long after such lessons the congregation noticed the quality of my voice, and the business man was pleased! My voice now had resonance. I could pitch my voice and change the tone and rhythm. I am deeply indebted to that dear lady. I wish she or someone like her were available now. I still use Vaseline before I preach!

The preacher reflects.

My best thoughts and ideas arrive in my mind during late nights or early mornings, often while lying in bed. It must be God's way of communicating with me! There are times when I wish I could stop the ideas from penetrating my mind and get some sleep! I find myself getting out of bed, going to my study, turning on the computer, and recording such thoughts and ideas before forgetting them.

A time of day I enjoy reflecting is prior to supper (that's what we farmers still call it instead of dinner!). I am privileged to have a home where the backyard faces a range of mountains. I love birds and feed them. I sit out on the patio with something to sip and on occasion smoke a cigar! (Yeah, I'm a bad boy, at times!) I look at the mountains and watch the birds eat, and thank the Lord for His creation. I find myself talking with God aloud. Fortunately, neighbors can't hear me! I find myself spending an hour or more doing this. It has become a time of restful relaxation and a time to answer such questions as these: What did I accomplish today? What am I going to do tomorrow? What about world conditions with its violence? What am I doing for others? What about that homeless woman I saw walking down the street pushing a grocery cart containing all her possessions?

Every person needs time to reflect and make some thoughtful decisions. I conclude the world would be a better place if people stopped whizzing around and took an inventory of themselves and the world.

The preacher exercises.

I am fortunate enough to belong to an athletic club with exercise machines, a pool, a spa, and a sauna. I lift weights every other day and walk the other days. Usually I play golf once a week.

Without thought of advertising, I bought food from Nutrisystems to help me re-think about what and how much I eat. I step on the scales regularly!

I am not saying my regimen is the best. I am no authority on health. I am simply saying the effort to stay healthy is good stewardship. Furthermore, Christians need to set an example by living a life that promotes good health. Come to think of it, I need to write a sermon on physical, mental, and spiritual health! All three dimensions of life are essential for preaching sincerely. I may have strayed a bit but I am keenly interested in the quality of life, especially among older people. Of course, I have good genes. My mother lived to be 108 ½ years old!

The preacher rehearses.

After a preacher finishes the manuscript of a sermon, the preacher is not finished. The preacher rehearses. After finishing a manuscript I always try preaching it with a recorder in my hand. I even went so far as to produce home videos of myself preaching! I was surprised by the way I looked and the gestures made. I asked myself this question: Would I become interested enough to listen to this guy?! (I never got an honest answer!)

A Hollywood movie producer once invited me to witness the filming of a scene that later appeared in the movie *Return of the Planet Apes*, back some distance into the Santa Monica Mountains in the Malibu area. Unfortunately Charlton Heston wasn't present! Present were several hundred people who looked and acted like apes plus others who were human victims. The director made them rehearse again and again and again one little scene until he could cry "cut," and the scene was judged good enough to be included in the movie. The scene included apes stomping the earth as if it would shake. The apes shrieked until my ears hurt. There was a war going on between apes and human beings and they were throwing people into cages. It was frightening!

Suddenly, at the end of the last scene toward the end of the day, an ape made a bee-line toward me! I cringed. The ape asked me a question: "Could you give me a lift back into town?" Fortunately, I could say "no" because I was going in a different direction. He was too realistic for me!

The preacher, in order to be effective, must be realistic. This requires rehearsal after rehearsal after rehearsal before appearing before a congregation.

The preacher speaks understandably.

I always had doubts about the necessity of "children's sermons." Can't children understand the "main" sermon? I have heard adults exclaim, "I get more out of children's sermons than I do out of main sermons!"

I am not decrying children's sermons. They are necessary. I am decrying the poor use of language in main sermons.

In the reading of Jesus' sermons I am always amazed at His conciseness and clarity. Even children listened. "Then he took a little child and put it among them; and taking it in his arms, he said to them, 'Whoever welcomes one such child in my name welcomes me, and whoever welcomes me welcomes not me but the one who sent me' " (Mark 9:36-37). I think that child understood! I always wondered what happened to that child.

Our preaching need not be esoteric: only for the ears of the educated and elite. Sermons need to be simple enough as to be understood by a child. Being "simple" does not mean stupid; it means being clear.

In preparing a sermon manuscript I strive for three things: cogency, clarity, and conciseness.

Once I gave a sermon manuscript to a friend who was having difficulty believing. I thought the manuscript addressed that question. After reading it his comment was, "It didn't do anything for me." I went back through that manuscript and found it failed the "three things" test noted above, and re-wrote it.

Words are not only precious; they are priceless bringing knowledge and insight. And sermons need to require a response. The eternal destiny of lives hangs in the balance. It is that serious.

+

I don't have an earned doctorate or even an honorary one! All I have is some knowledge and worldwide experiences. I am just an ordinary pastor with years of experience in the pulpit (since 1944). I don't consider myself a great preacher. I do think I am a responsible herald of the Word. You be the judge! I hope these "timeless lifetime sermons" help someone come to Christ and His church. That's the hook! That's my purpose in providing these sermons in print.

Sermon 1

Chief Obstacle of the Church

Text: Exodus 6-15

Moses said to the people, "Do not be afraid, stand firm, and see the deliverance that the Lord will accomplish for you today"...Then the Lord said to Moses, "... Tell the Israelites to go forward."

— Exodus 14:13, 15

What would you say is the greatest obstacle of the church today? Secularism? Agnosticism? Other religions? Social Issues?

Scripture sheds light on these questions. Insight is obtainable by a glimpse at the circumstances surrounding Moses and the Israelites during their first taste of freedom.

The Israelites had been slaves of the Egyptians spanning a generation, some forty years. Slavery does something to a people. Older people lose hope. Younger people lack vision. The crack of a whip can mean not only a slice in a person's flesh but it can mean the mind whipped into a frame of futility. A day's labor for an Israelite was often taking the place of a beast at a wheel grinding grain or carrying huge stones for the altar of an idol.

God saw all this. He did not permit people to remain in bondage. God sent a messenger, a man with a checkered past and who stammered. The man was Moses.

Standing in the Court of the Pharaoh, Moses announced the plan of God to let His people go into a promised land. The Pharaoh did not believe in Moses' God nor His power.

By God's instruction, Moses lifted his hand and plagues occurred afflicting the Egyptian people. The plagues included turning water into blood, frogs, gnats, flies, disease of livestock, boils, thunder and hail, and locusts. Pharaoh promised again and

31

again that if a plague were lifted, he would allow the Israelites to go. He was a liar. He broke eight promises.

God tired of this procedure. He instructed Moses to tell the people to make a sacrifice and in the process to place the blood of the sacrificed lamb upon their doorposts as an outward sign of belief in God. During the night an angel of the Lord would pass over all the homes of Egypt. The homes without the blood of a lamb on the doorpost would suffer the loss of the first-born of the family.

During the night, wailing and lamentation occurred in the homes of the Egyptians, including the palace of the Pharaoh, as the angel passed over their homes. Their first-born were slain.

The next morning there was an outcry by the Egyptians. They pleaded with the Pharaoh to allow the Israelites to go. The Pharaoh finally said to Moses, "Rise up, go away from my people, both you and the Israelites! Go, worship the Lord, as you said. Take your flocks and your herds, as you said, and be gone. And bring a blessing on me too!" (Exodus 12:31-32).

Moses and his brother, Aaron, gathered the Israelites together, 600,000 (the count included men only), the women and the children. The Israelites began the journey to the Promised Land with their flocks and herds.

They came to the edge of the Red Sea, having journeyed into the wilderness. Looking behind them, at a distance, they saw dust swirling into the sky. It took no imagination to realize what was occurring. The Egyptians were pursuing. The Pharaoh had changed his mind once again, not believing in a blessing from God. He took things into his own hands. After all, he had the greatest army in the known world, with 600 chariots, and he did not believe in a blessing from God. The Israelites could see their armor glistening in the sun, and they could almost feel the point of swords piercing their flesh. They were frightened to death!

They complained to Moses. "Was it because there were no graves in Egypt that you have taken us away to die in the wilderness? What have you done to us, bringing us out of Egypt? Is this not the very thing we told you in Egypt, 'Let us alone and let us serve the Egyptians?' For it would have been better for us to serve the Egyptians than to die in the wilderness" (Exodus 14:11-12).

Moses replied: "Do not be afraid, stand firm and see the deliverance that the Lord will accomplish for you today" (Exodus 14:13). However, Moses was not too sure himself about the result. He went behind a rock and asked God, "What do I do now?!" God said, "Tell the people to go forward."

A pillar of cloud came to hide them from the Egyptians. Moses stretched out his hand over the sea and God caused a strong east wind that parted the waves during the night. It took faith for the people to walk in that path provided by God. When they walked forward the east wind kept the waters back!

Egyptians pursued. But their chariot wheels became clogged in the mud. Moses, with the people now safely across the sea, extended his hand again, as directed by God, and the east wind ceased. The sea returned drowning the Pharaoh and all his men. Not one Egyptian warrior escaped. The people of Israel knelt in the sand, prayed, and sang, "The Lord is my strength and my might..." (Exodus 15:2).

What was the chief obstacle of the Israelites? The Egyptians? The Sea? No. It was the danger that the Israelites would not respond to God's word spoken by Moses. The greatest miracle of that day was not the parting of the waves; it was the God-given faith that took the Israelites through a path to safe land, with bays of water on both sides of them.

Now, we are ready to ask the question again: What is the church's chief obstacle today?

Secularism? Yes, it is a danger because secularism teaches that we should "eat, drink, and be merry" without thought of tomorrow. It teaches the separation of everyday life from any connection with God. Secularism is a danger that should not be minimized. But, it is not the greatest danger.

Agnosticism? It is a real danger. It teaches that the ultimate cause and the essential nature of things are unknown or unknowable. Self-made intellects are dangerous. But, agnosticism, with its accusations, is not the greatest danger.

Other Religions? Other religions are human created for the purpose of fulfilling human needs. People with personal problems can be soothed by clever statements. For example, in this country the Science of Mind sects are concoctions by people (Ron

Hubbard). In other countries, Islam extremists threaten the world. All these religions are a danger but they are not the greatest danger to the Christian church.

Social issues? Christian churches do not seem to know how to handle the issue of homosexuality. The way people have sex in a bedroom has become the topic of the day. Some make their case based on their interpretation of scripture. It is true that homosexuality doesn't lead anywhere except to personal satisfaction for certain people who knowingly choose to have sex a different way. The propagation of human life is not important to homosexuals. Personal satisfaction is their goal. All of this bickering about homosexuality is a danger but it is not the greatest danger to the Christian church of today.

The chief obstacle of the Christian church, like that of the Israelites at the Red Sea, is the danger that church people will not hearken, will not listen, will not respond to the word of God.

The word of God says: "Go therefore and make disciples of all nations...." (Matthew 28:19). The word of God says: "Go, stand in the temple and tell the people the whole message about this life" (Acts 5:20). The word of God reports: "Then Phillip began to speak, and starting with this scripture, he proclaimed to him the good news about Jesus" (Acts 8:35). The word of God reports Peter saying: "I have no silver or gold, but what I have I give you: in the name of Jesus Christ of Nazareth, stand up and walk" (Acts 3:6). The word of God says: "All of them were filled with the Holy Spirit, and began to speak in other languages, as the Spirit gave them ability" (Acts 2:4).

The church of today has the same word of God. The church has the Word and the Sacraments. The church has available the same power. The chief danger is failing to utilize the resources of God.

James S. Stewart of Scotland said it for me: "The fact remains that the greatest drag on Christianity today, the most serious menace to the church's mission, is not the secularism without, it is the reduced Christianity within (*Heralds of God*, p. 17).

Christians who bear the stamp of Christ need to realize they are on urgent business. Christians are never to think of themselves as some little subcommittee indulging in trivial matters. They are not news reporters making commonplace announcements. Rather, they are the King's spokespersons. They are to remember what the King said, "You did not choose me, but I chose you. And I appointed you to go and bear fruit, fruit that will last..." (John 15:17).

God has appointed the church to bear fruit. It involves making visible to the world the acts of God. It involves introducing people to God in Christ so that people can have a right relationship with God.

God provides a path for every person. God pushes back waves of indifference and inertia. God's people then begin to understand why they were created, what their purpose in life is, and learn to sing the song of salvation.

God used Moses, a murderer and a stammerer. God can use any person who will respond to His word: "Do not be afraid, stand firm, and see the deliverance that the Lord will accomplish for you today.... Tell the people to go forward!"

Sermon 2

The Circle of Redemption

Text: John 16

> "I came from the father and have come into the world; again, I am leaving the world and going to the father."
>
> — John 16:28

Are you on the right road? It has been said of old that there are many roads that lead to God. The inference is it doesn't matter which religion you choose as long as you let God know you are on the way!

This reminds me of the Nebraska postman visiting Los Angeles for the first time getting lost on the Hollywood Freeway for eight hours! Millions of people are lost on "some" road to God. The signs of human religions lead them on a detour. The multiplicity of churches in Christianity confuses some and causes them to insist on going their own way.

I say to you that John 16:28 is a tested statement declaring there is only one road that leads to God, a road that originates in eternity and comes from above, continues into the world, and returns to heaven.

This statement of our Lord in John 16:28 could be called "the circle of redemption." It is not simply a circle that goes round and round but a circle comprehending the nature of God. In ecclesiastical language it is the Incarnation, the Crucifixion, the Resurrection, and the Ascension of our Lord.

We often speak of living on the straight and narrow path. Redemption is a word that describes our predicament — people in need of a right relationship with their maker. This circle of redemption may have the perspective of being straight. It took a Columbus to show earthbound people that the world was round and not flat. It took Jesus Christ to redeem us. With eyes of faith we can see Jesus' circle. He shares the imperfections of human beings and the perfectness of God.

This circle of redemption began in heaven. Jesus said, "I came from the Father." It is difficult for us to comprehend Jesus' existence from the beginning of time. Nevertheless, John in his first chapter writes, "In the beginning was the Word, and the Word was with God, and the Word was God."

Listen to the testimony of scripture concerning Jesus' preexistence before birth as a child in Bethlehem: "No one has ever seen God. It is God the only Son, who is close to the Father's heart, who has made him known" (John 1:18). "No one has ascended into heaven except the one who descended from heaven, the Son of Man" (John 3:13). "For I have come down from heaven, not to do my own will, but the will of him who sent me" (John 6:38). "… Very truly, I tell you, before Abraham was, I am" (John 8:58). "… Father, glorify me in your presence with the glory I had in your presence before the world existed" (John 17:5).

A boy in our elementary school asked the question, "Who made God?" The answer is nobody made God. The same question can be asked of Christ. God the Father, God the Son existed from the beginning. They are one. Nothing existed before God.

All things come from God. We need to acknowledge what comes from the Father. We should thank God for all creation. We should thank Him for food, shelter, clothing, work, and pleasure. We should thank Him for joys of this life and the strength to endure troubles. Many have learned to ask and to receive as John 16:23 suggests: "On that day you will ask nothing of me. Very truly, I tell you, if you ask anything of the Father in my name, he will give it to you."

We need to thank the Father for the Son. Think what it meant for the Son to be sent:

Divinity to take on humanity;
Omnscience to become a child;
Omnipotence to become arms and legs;
King to become servant!

John stated Jesus' words, "I came from the Father." Certainly it is God's greatest miracle. It trumpeted the day when all human misery will end.

When Jesus said, "I came from the Father and have come into the world," He was saying the Incarnation was necessary. If God created a new world for human beings still under the domination of evil, it would mean human beings would have another opportunity to plant hell on earth. The destruction of human beings in Noah's time is sufficient evidence for this occurrence.

No one can say they willed to be born. Only Christ can say that. Christ chose to be born. The Incarnation was the confrontation of a lost humanity with God's redeeming love.

Some have detoured on the road to redemption when addressing the virgin birth. We believe in the virgin birth or our confession in the creeds is a mockery. We cannot eradicate part of the creed and still have our faith. Unless Christ came as a human being, how could He identify Himself with the human race?

We deny the roads created by human minds that deny the virgin birth. Walter Barlow wrote in his book *God so Loved*, "May God give us tolerance when tolerance means reverence for the right of others to think freely but God save us from the fatal delusion that we shall ever see the world redeemed from its sin by a religious emulsion compounded of all the brands of religion on earth" (pp. 44-45).

Christ came into our world. We believe in a historical Jesus and a heaven sent Jesus! He laid aside His divine power following the Upper Room experience. Paul wrote in Philippians 2:7-8, "… Being found in human form, he humbled himself and became obedient to the point of death — even death on a cross."

Jesus said in this text that He was leaving the world. Christ not only chose to be born but He chose to die. He had "… the power to lay it down" (John 10:18). No one took His life; He gave it! His death completes His identification with humankind.

Christ also chose to be resurrected. He had the "… power to take it up again" (John 10:18). The scripture doesn't say that an angel unwrapped His garments while He was in the tomb. The power of rising from the dead was His divine nature. His resurrection is the demonstration that death is not the end for believers.

Christ chose to ascend. He did not require angels to bear Him upon their wings. There was no multiple rocket system to carry Him into outer space. Christ alone had the power to ascend.

Do you see this "circle of redemption"? Christ left disciples well equipped to carry on the Good News! Behind Him, Christ left forces of goodness more powerful than the forces of evil. Christ left a road leading to eternal life.

Human beings experience the force of evil and the power of God. A loving Christ leads us against the foe. The Word of God sustains and inspires us. The promise of a two-stage life becomes a reality.

This "circle of redemption" is completed with the Ascension of Christ. Christ completed the circle: from the Father, into the world, and to the Father in heaven. Now Christ is elevated to the highest. He fills the hearts of human beings with faith and imagination so that we desire a heavenly home.

At a graveside we look into a dark cavity and wonder. But we need not wonder anymore. Christ completed the circle of eternity. He is at the "... right hand of God." Where He is, His believers will be.

We look up into the sky and think of the disciples standing on a mountain watching Christ ascend. What a road to travel! That is also our destiny. We go to God on Judgment Day!

Does this not touch your imagination? Does this thought inspire you to live a Christian life, not for the reward at the end of the road, but for the continual joy along the road with the living Christ?

John 16:28 and the Creeds are reciprocally related. When Christ proclaimed where He came from and where He was going, He made a statement of faith. The Creeds only expound the proclamation.

These convictions expressed by Christ are sufficient to help us in our infirmities, strong enough to deliver us, and powerful enough to lift us onto the road to eternity.

Are you on the right road? There is no second chance after death. The gate is narrow. The way is hard as Matthew 7:13 expresses it: "Enter through the narrow gate; for the gate is wide and the road is easy that leads to destruction, and there are many who take it." There is no promise of immunity from the calamities of life. God does not offer a pillow but He does offer a promise, "... Enter into the joy of your master" (Matthew 25:21).

Will you find the road? Here it is: "I came from the Father and have come into the world; again, I am leaving the world and going to the Father" (John 16:28). Belief in the resurrected Jesus is the road to eternity!

Sermon 3

A Hell There Is

Text: Luke 16:19-31

In Hades, where he was being tormented, he looked up and saw Abraham far away with Lazarus by his side. He called out, "Father Abraham, have mercy on me, and send Lazarus to dip the tip of his finger in water and cool my tongue; for I am in agony in these flames."

— Luke 16:22-24

Few people seem to take seriously this parable of our Lord. Many do not know how to interpret this scripture. Literalists think the parable is a description of hell. The modernist thinks there is no hell. "After all," a man candidly remarked to me, "How could a good God stand to see people suffer in a flame of fire for the remainder of their days?" Briefly, it seems we have traded the preaching of hell and brimstone days for the adult western!

This parable is not a description of Satan's territory. As a matter of fact, nobody can tell you what hell is really like since no one has come back from the dead to tell us! Contrary to what some people claim, scripture does not describe the temperature of heaven or hell. Furthermore, it doesn't make any difference whether hell is a fire or a cold freeze! What makes a difference is what kind of life you live here. What makes a difference is believing we are to live with God forever. It certainly would be hell to live without God's love and goodness, now and forever!

Our Lord in this parable takes a rabbinical teaching of Hades and points out to proud Pharisees that what a person does with what he has reveals the kind of person he is, and what happens to him.

What kind of a person was this man, often called "Dives," which means "rich"? He had fine clothes and good eats. He had an estate with a gate. If he lived today, I would picture him living in a gated community in a house with a view, built around a swimming pool, and belonging to an exclusive country club playing golf every day.

Actually, I am describing the kind of house I would enjoy and the kind of life I would lead if I had the chance! You can imagine what you think it means to be rich on this earth. Dives had it made!

The scripture doesn't tell us the temperament Dives had, the kind of moral life he lived, or whether he was tall or short in stature. It only says he was "… dressed in purple and fine linen and who feasted sumptuously every day." Come to think of it, I always liked the color purple!

Some like to accuse Jesus of berating riches and lauding the status of the poor. They cannot do that. Dives was not damned because he lived well but because he ignored Lazarus. Dives' sin was being a selfish, self-centered person.

Frequently, a rich man is above average in intelligence. If a person inherits money, he needs brains to manage it. The *Los Angeles Times* (5-29-59) reported that a man spurned money due him from the government because, he said, "It is nothing but a nuisance."

Regardless of how much money you have, rich or poor, failure to share what you have is sin.

"Lazaraus" means "God is help." It is symbolic to say that Dives means "help yourself." Lazarus was under the nose of Dives. Dives couldn't help seeing his plight. There was no excuse. Because the dogs, considered unclean animals, licked the sores of Lazarus indicates that Lazarus was helpless. Lazarus asked Dives for help in his plight.

Did you ever think that Dives could have been the answer to prayer? That he could have been an instrument of God? Instead, Dives contributed to the death of Lazarus. Dives was so concerned with his own affairs, with his own estate interests, he left the man to die.

If a person ignores what he sees, you can be sure he will ignore what he cannot see. It is not only our duty to help deserving people around us, the good and the bad, people who need help, but it is also our duty to help the charities of the community and the world. The Christian needs to act when a plea comes to help the hungry and the homeless, and those who need medical attention, and those who need attention.

I do not know the kind of life comedian Bud Abbott lived, but when he lost his money he complained that his friends left him. Lazarus felt that way in his dying days.

Jesus' parable says that Lazarus and Dives died. Riches cannot save you from the grave. All people, in God's time, must die and be judged. Jesus said the selfish, self-centered man went to hell.

Dives sent a message from hell. His message consisted of requests. First, he asked for a drop of water on his tongue. He was in conversation with Abraham. Abraham reminded him that he had his days of sumptuous living and disregarded God and people. Dives was told this was the necessary end to a selfish life. But, Dives pleaded for help and note this, help from the very man he spurned in his own lifetime! Abraham continued, "Besides all this, between you and us a great chasm has been fixed so that those who might want to pass from here to you cannot do so, and no one can cross from there to us."

Dives was told that he had disregarded God. This was the act of a sinful person; not God's choosing. "It is impossible to receive a drop of water, Dives. You had your chance. You refused God."

It might seem Dives became evangelistic. His second request was to help his five brothers. Evidently, they were living the same kind of life he had lived. Dives was really saying that if he had known, he would have done differently.

See how human beings are! They endeavor to shift the blame on God! Dives tries to blame his condition on insufficient warnings. The real fault of human beings is not God's failure to give warnings but human beings' failure to heed God's testimony given through His servants throughout the ages.

Abraham said to Dives: "They have Moses and the prophets; let them hear them." But Dives didn't pay any attention to God's word spoken by the prophets. If he had, he would not have remained self-centered, caught in the same trap as Adam and Eve, and unwilling to be changed by God.

Today, people have the testimony of Paul and the church. "The cross is a signpost to every person. It points the way for him to take the road of life from the cradle to the grave. In Great Britain, after the battle of Dunkirk, in World War II, the signs at the crossroads were taken down. Fearing an invasion from the enemy by parachute, they removed the signs to confuse them. But the people of Great Britain became confused, and many lost their way because the familiar sentinels were down at the crossroads" (*Evangelism in a Changing America*, Jesse Bader, pp. 34-35).

Could it be that the cross is ignored by those caught in the mainstream of making a living, tripped by their own bundle of activity, that they are detoured by their insistence of discovering their own way of life?

The cross is the testimony today. They have Christ and His cross. Let them hear Him!

Dives was uncertain they would listen. "These people want proof, you know. They are intelligent people. If you send someone from the dead, they will repent. That's all they need — positive proof!"

Abraham replied, "If they hear not Moses and the prophets, neither will they be persuaded, though one rose from the dead."

How modern are the pleas of Dives. There is the person in his gated community overlooking the beauty of nature and overlooking the plight of people. There is the person in his heated swimming pool and his neighbor swimming in polite idolatry. There is a person at the table forgetting the table of the Lord which says, "God is help." There is a person providing a pound of meat for his dog and not providing an ounce of help for his neighbor!

"Send somebody from the dead and they will repent." "Send somebody to explain what the scripture says." "Send somebody to tell us what is Christian and which way to follow."

Our Lord replies, "I died for you. The church has the Word and the Sacraments. Information talks are available for visitors to attend where they can hear the whole story. Bible classes are available where they can study my word. Everyone of you repent and be baptized. Put a cross in your heart and an eye on heaven."

Who are these people who demand evidence? What evidence will they believe? Put the script of the gospel in television language and focus the camera on a fiery pit. Will people believe? Fear has never saved anyone. Only faith can save. God can implant faith in any heart willing to hear and receive.

44

We need to become realistic about the terrible nature of self-centeredness and its consequence. Dives' message from hell should stir our minds and shake our wills. Look up and not down. Behold Lazarus there with Abraham. The saints did not demand justice or proof but lived in faith. You can't live on bread alone. You can't live by wearing fancy clothes. You can't live in a walled community forever. You can't live selfishly and be saved. You can live by faith.

God help us to see our own need at our nose. God help us keep our sights low enough and high enough to see the needs at home and around the world. People are not saved by what they think but by God who can direct and re-direct humankind's thinking. The rich Christian and the poor Christian can be taken by God's angels into Abraham's bosom!

Sermon 4

Lessons at a Lake

Text: Luke 5:1-11

"When they had brought their boats to shore, they left everything and followed him."

— Luke 5:11

The Lake of Gennesaret or the Sea of Galilee is a heart-shaped fresh water lake in north Palestine, and an integral part of the Jordan River waterway. The Bible describes it by various names. It is approximately thirteen miles long and eight miles wide and is 680 feet below sea level. Its greatest depth is approximately 200 feet. The east side has 2,000 foot high mountains rising abruptly from its shores. The west side mountains are less abrupt. The fertile garden plains of Gennesaret are toward the north. The waters of the Jordan River empty into the lake and come from snow-capped Mount Hermon. Villages surround the lake or sea.

This Lake of Gennesaret was the scene of an early morning teaching experience of our Lord "… as the crowd was pressing in on him to hear the word of God." The crowd was so large that Jesus asked Peter's permission to get into his boat so that the crowd could come closer.

The teaching, however, did not stop at the shore. The greatest lessons were yet to come. Jesus did not perform a miracle for the crowd. The multitude did not get to witness a great fishing event. Our Lord saved the miracle of the draught of fishes for four men who later became His disciples.

What lessons did these four men learn that day — lessons we all need to learn?

One of the lessons was obedience.

Jesus invited these men to go fishing. Peter said, "Master, we have worked all night long but have caught nothing." This was a natural reaction. Didn't Peter know more about fishing than Jesus? Jesus was only a carpenter. Peter was certain it was useless to fish again since he and his companions, Andrew, James, and John, were unsuccessful during a whole night of fishing.

Surprisingly, Peter uttered necessary words, "Yet, if you say so, I will let down the nets." Why did Peter say that? They had been up all night, lowering and pulling up nets without landing a single fish. Breakfastless, nets already half cleaned, sleepy, and tired — they could have refused the request of Jesus to launch out into the deep and let down their nets again. "Yet, if you say so...."

They obeyed out of love and respect for Jesus. These four men were not depressed by past failure or afraid to try again. At Christ's word they obeyed.

Obedience is a matter of trust and goes out into the deep. Who would be willing to go out into 200 feet deep waters with a person unwilling to be obedient? Who would entrust his life in the troubled waters of life to a person tired of trying to be Christian?

Respect and love for Christ prompted Peter to take Jesus at His word. When you obey out of love and respect, you do not fear fresh toil.

You and I need the kind of obedience motivated by love and respect. The person who works hard all week and complains that Sunday is his only day off and is too tired to worship cannot be trusted to launch into the deep. The person who is depressed by recent failure and will not take God's word cannot be trusted to venture into deep waters. The person who shirks church work because of things left undone at home cannot be trusted to venture forth into the deep.

People who obey God's word, motivated by the love of Christ, launch out! You who have sinned and cannot see the importance of obedience, let down your net for a draught! You who have toiled all night on your own enterprise, accept our Lord's invitation to go with Him in the early hours of the morning and toil again.

Like Peter, who thought there would be no fish to catch, we are tempted to disregard a carpenter. What does Christ know about my situation? Say with Peter those important words, "Yet, if you say so...." I will go.

John Henry Jowett, once the pastor of the Fifth Avenue Presbyterian Church in New York City, said this about the constraint of Christ's love: "Here is a new constraint. The love of Christ hurries me along like a cloud. I am taken up in its mighty movement and stretched along the appointed road, for it arrests me and makes me its willing prisoner. It lays a strong hand upon me and gives me no option but to go. The man who is the prisoner of the Lord's love will find himself in new and wonderful scenery. Everything will wear a new face — God, man, self, the garden, the sky, and trees. We shall look at all things with love's eyes."

That's what happened to Peter, Andrew, James, and John. Obedience was the first step. Having love and respect for the Master, they launched out into the deep. We also can launch out.

Another lesson is to acknowledge the presence of God in the present.

Both boats went out into the deep. Both boats were soon filled with fish. Peter quicky perceived what had happened. He fell down at Jesus' knees and cried out, "Go away from me, Lord, for I am a sinful man!" Peter is struck by God's immediate presence. This was a miracle! Peter had seen Jesus perform miracles, but here in his own boat the impact of Christ's presence overwhelmed him and said not "master" but "Lord."

These words describe the feeling of a person who is confronted with divine power. Peter became fearful. He finds himself in the presence of what Otto called "the wholly other." Peter finds himself face-to-face with something outside and beyond and different from himself, something he cannot fully understand.

What was Peter's reaction? He had a quick sense of sin and recoiled in terror. In recognition of Christ as God, Peter recognized his own sin. "Go away from me, Lord, for I am a sinful man." Peter must have thought punishment comes when the perfect Christ meets an imperfect person.

A person realizes sin when confronted with God's nearness. If you are self-centered, you reject the presence of God in your life. If you live superficially, your life cannot be pierced by the presence of God. Life can be punctuated with God's presences when you differentiate right from wrong.

Peter felt uneasy with Christ in his boat. He mistakenly felt, for a moment, he would be safer if he were not near the Master.

But, Peter, even if Christ is not there the facts remain the same. Simply because the Physician departs does not mean the disease also departs.

We commit the same error by trying to eradicate thoughts that make us uncomfortable. We have the power to overlook circumstances we like to ignore. Pretense will not help. Scripture states, "for as he thinketh in his heart" so is he (King James, Proverbs 23:7).

People immerse themselves in work or plunge into some pleasure to get rid of troublesome thoughts. It is true your conscience will stop speaking if you shut God out. Remember truth does not cease to be truth because we refuse to look at it. If you drown truth with a closed mind, you do not change truth but yourself. Facts still remain.

In a little book titled *The Screwtape Letters*, a devil reports to headquarters telling how he diverted a man from God. Deep in thought in a London library, the man was becoming convinced that God, the very God, had dealings with him. The man kept saying, "Thou." He knew the mystery of the word: the vast and lonely cosmos seemed to give very little warrant for it. But he kept saying it, "Thou." How, then, did the devil divert him? Not by argument: devils wisely know that nothing can be proved or disproved by argument. No, the devil touched the man on the shoulder of his thoughts, saying: "Aren't you feeling hungry? It's nearly lunch time." So he got the man out of doors where he could see the Number 73 bus rumbling on its way and hear the newsboys shouting, "Extra!" Soon the man was earthbound once more, wondering how he could have been such a fool as to be exorcised by God (cited by George Buttrick, *Sermons Preached in a University*, p. 147).

Peter's solution was in the boat. His first reaction was superficial. Superficial knowledge can drive us from Christ. Deeper convictions draw us to Jesus. Later in life Peter exclaimed, "Lord, to whom can we go? You have the words of eternal life. We have come to believe and know that you are the Holy One of God" (John 6:67-68).

Still another lesson Jesus taught: the ultimate purpose in life.

The greatest achievement of the day was not the draught of fish. "When they had brought their boats to shore, they left everything and followed him" (Luke 5:11). The fishing occupation was abandoned. The four men followed our Lord. This was the greatest catch of the day! Our Lord netted people of devotion and determination.

This does not mean they never went fishing again or never saw their families and friends again. It does mean that Peter, Andrew, James, and John discovered the ultimate purpose in life — to catch people for the kingdom.

A church can be compared to a post office. Each post office requires many duties but one principle requirement — to deliver the mail.

A new post office was erected in one of our large cities during the great Depression. At that time it was reported to be one of the most complete post offices in America. There were abundant facilities. There were all types of departments including the most modern mechanical devices to speed the mails to their rightful destinations. There were even special slots to deposit air mail, R.F.D. letters, special deliveries, and so on.

The most prominent Washington officials were present for the elaborately planned dedication ceremony. When the ceremonies were to begin, someone wanted to deposit what was then the first three-cent letter. They discovered there was no letter drop for ordinary mail. They had made meticulous provision for everything else but made no provision for the main business of a post office, simple ordinary letters. (Gleaned from *Building Church Membership Through Evangelism* by Bryan, p. 31.)

The church's main purpose is the ordinary mail — leading people to Christ. The Christian's ultimate purpose is to lead someone to Christ and His church. I doubt if you know what Christianity is about if you have never led someone to Christ. There would be more Christians in the world today if there were less lobbying in the narthex and more laboring in the vineyard!

When preaching on an evangelism mission in Hawaii, I learned how they used to catch fish in Hawaii. Several men of the village were responsible for setting nets in the lagoon. These men yelled when they saw fish coming: "Houkilau, Houkilau" and the villagers came running, each taking his place by a net and together pulling in the net containing fish. The nets were set again. Again, when the appointed men saw fish coming, they cried out, "Houkilau, Houkilau" and the villagers came running, each taking a place by the net, and together they pulled in the net containing fish.

The church should be like that. The Evangelism Committee could set the nets. They could cry out, "Houkilau, Houkilau" when a series of Information Talks for Visitors was to be given, and all members of the church could come running: Council, committees, organizations, choirs, instrumentalists, the young and the older, everyone taking his place by the net inviting people to the info talks. That is how to catch people for Christ and His church.

Don't call a preacher and put him/her on probation by saying, "Well, let's give him/her a few months or even a year and see what he/she can do." You can't shift your Christian responsibility in calling a pastor to do what the Lord has called you to do.

By obedience to His word, with Christ by our side, and by His power, people can be caught in the net of the Word and the Sacraments.

Sermon 5

Parable of the Elder Brother

Text: Luke 15:11-32

"But the elder brother was out in the fields, and as he came near the house, he heard music and dancing. So he called one of the servants across to him and enquired what was the meaning of it all. 'Your brother has arrived, and your father has killed the calf we fattened because he has got him home again safe and sound,' was the reply. But he was furious and refused to go inside the house. So his father came outside and called to him. Then he burst out, 'Look, how many years have I slaved for you and never disobeyed a single order of yours and yet you have never given me so much as a young goat, so that I could give my friends a dinner? But when that son of yours arrives, who has spent all your money on prostitutes, for him you kill the calf we've fattened!' But the father replied, 'My son, you have been with me all the time and everything I have is yours. But we had to celebrate and show our joy. For this is your brother; I thought he was dead — and he's alive. I thought he was lost — and he is found!'"

— Phillips translation

Dictionaries describe a parable as a short story "… based on a familiar experience and having an application to the spiritual life…." The parables of our Lord represent the highest development of this narrative form (*Harper's Dictionary*, p. 521).

Jesus used this form of teaching to illustrate spiritual truths. He does so in this parable of the Elder Brother as well as in the parable of the Prodigal Son, which precedes it. Both illustrate truths Jesus intended.

The parable of the Prodigal Son is more easily understood. We understand it well because it paints a clear picture of sin in its naked form, a person sunk in the depths of degradation.

52

The younger son asked for his inheritance and received it. He wanted to see how the rest of the world lived since he lived on a farm. He wanted to be his own master. Away from his father's eye, he experienced every fleshly impulse. Essentially, the prodigal son who left home was a self-centered individual and riotous living came natural. However, he soon discovered that a godless world is hard and cold. Godless people don't care for anyone but themselves. With all his inheritance spent, the prodigal found himself among the swine.

Scripture states, "He came to himself." Did he return home because of conscience? No. Was it because of his love for his father the prodigal returned? No. His stomach was the reason for his return home. "And when he came to himself, he said, 'How many hired servants of my father's have bread enough and to spare, and I perish with hunger!' "

The prodigal decided to go home. Each step toward home must have become harder. I wonder if the prodigal would have made it if he had to make his way past servants to reach his father and confess all?! But the father saw him coming! Paternal love is like that. The more God's love is poured out the more we feel our own sin. Love never dies. The father not only saw him coming but ran out to meet him. After the boy's confession there is silence. The father puts a robe on him, symbol of home, so that the marks of the sin country experience could be covered. A ring was placed on his finger, symbol of sonship. Shoes were put on his feet. In contrast slaves went barefoot. The son must have shoes for the journey in life. A feast was prepared so all could rejoice, "For this is your brother; I thought he was dead — and he's alive. I thought he was lost — and he is found."

This is a picture of God forgiving a penitent sinner. God is ready and eager to forgive and restore the sinner. Remember the hymn: "For the love of God is broader than the measure of man's mind, And the heart of the Eternal is most wonderfully kind."

What was the reaction of the elder brother when his prodigal brother came home? Coming in late from a hard day's work in the field, hearing music and dancing, he asked one of the servants what was happening. Upon being told his brother had returned, the fatted calf was killed, and everybody was rejoicing, "He was angry, and would not go in...." Phillips translation puts it stronger: "But he was furious and refused to go into the house."

The prodigal was not the only sinner or the worst sinner. "The hardest people to reach," said Charles Allen in *The Heart Is Hungry* "with the love of God are not the bad people. They know they are bad. They have no defense. The hardest ones to win for God are the self-righteous people" (p. 37).

The elder son had worked faithfully in the fields through the years and had obeyed his father's orders. But why? Did he work because he loved his father? No. Did he obey his father's orders because he respected his father? No. He slaved and obeyed through the years for what he could get out of it — material blessings.

The older son considered himself morally superior. The worse his brother became the better he felt. In his father's presence the older son tended to think to himself, "Aren't you thankful you have a son like I am and not like the strayed sheep of the family?"

Do you suppose he worried about his brother who had left home and was headed in the wrong direction? Do you suppose he ever prayed for his brother? Do you suppose he ever had a sleepless night worrying about his brother's welfare?

The father's heart had been broken. You know he worried; you know he prayed; you know he spent many a sleepless night worrying about his younger son.

The elder brother was unaware that you do not serve God to gain His material blessings. "... For he makes His sun shine on the evil and on the good, and sends rain on the righteous and on the unrighteous" (Matthew 5:45).

The elder brother did not believe that a wayward son could be welcomed home. There was no love in his heart. Instead of greeting his brother, he stayed outside and pouted.

The father did not neglect either son. "The father came out and began to plead..." with the older son (v. 26).

The answer of the elder brother to the gentle pleading of the father was a raging temper of unsparing condemnation. As Susan Ertz wrote in the novel *The Prodigal Heart*, "while the younger son was prodigal in body, at least part of his heart was always at home; but the elder brother was prodigal at heart, and only his body was at home" (cited by *Interpreter's*, p. 279).

The elder brother's pride choked concern for others. He was the kind of fellow who would say other races are inferior; that a person without a job is unemployable; that some people are hopeless; that a progressive mind is dangerous; that doubts if it pays to be good.

We need to say with Friedrich W. Krumacher (*ibid*, p. 279) as a questioner asked his opinion of the elder brother's identity, replied "I learned it only yesterday about myself."

In this parable, is Jesus talking about us? We need to ask ourselves that question. A small injection of religion makes us think discipleship means abstaining from life's pleasures, and in the struggle to sidestep the taint of sin build up a nice little split-level religion where we conclude that down below are the sinners; up here in the better part of town are the saints!

Is the church ever a prodigal at heart? What if a prodigal entered the church doors at the command of Jesus? Would members rejoice? What is the purpose of the church? To prosper or to find the lost? How many prodigals have been driven back into the far country by the lovelessness of good church people? Individuals as well as the church need to answer these questions.

Have you heard the story of the three sons? Two of them were sons of the earth; the other a Son in heaven, begotten not made. The younger son on earth forgot his true home and by fleshly desires sank into shame. The older son on earth, though not unmindful of home, began to despise his brother and so grew hard of heart through pride of mind. The Son of heaven sought the sons of the earth. He found the younger son among the husks and shared his shame but the prodigal was deaf: "No brother of mine," he cried, "and God is only a name."

So, the Son of God then found the elder prodigal who was in church but he also was hard of heart: "Why should you seek my brother?" he asked bitterly, "for he is a wastrel: you are no better than he." Then befell the most cruel thing earth has ever known: the two prodigals killed the Son of God. In the hate that yearning can bring they slew him on a cross. But, the Son of God prayed for them as He died. The younger prodigal said, "I would return to God if I had not killed his only-begotten Son, but now...." The older prodigal said: "I never knew my lovelessness until I saw His love, but I have killed Him, so now…." Then, the Son of God rose from the dead, for a grave could not imprison His great love, and both prodigals knew that He was with them. What they then did, who can say? You and I must choose the answer (*ibid*, p. 272).

Thank God both prodigals can be saved. "In Christ God was reconciling the world unto himself" (2 Corinthians 5:19).

Sermon 6

Parable of the
Friend at Midnight

Text: Luke 11:5-13

Bearing in mind that our Lord in telling a parable always was illustrating a truth, the parable of the friend at midnight shows the willingness of God to answer prayer.

The parable tells of a fellow who had an unexpected guest arrive at a very late hour. It was customary, in those times, to provide a meal for a guest regardless of the hour of arrival. Journeys were often made at night in order to avoid the heat of the day. But this host had no food! The cupboard was bare. What do you do in an event like that? It is night. There is no place to purchase food. Like the lady of the house, even in daytime, this host went next door to get food from a neighbor. "Friend, lend me three loaves of bread; for a friend of mine has arrived, and I have nothing to set before him."

A voice came from the inside, "Do not bother me; the door has already been locked, and my children are with me in bed; I cannot get up and give you anything."

Don't be too hard on the neighbor. Think of what it meant to get up at midnight. If he got up he would have to light a candle. The house was cold and who wants to get out of bed in the cold?! The children were asleep. Perhaps he had a hard time putting them to bed. If he got up the children would awaken and he would have a difficult time quieting the household again. So, the neighbor said, "Do not bother me...."

But, the neighbor did get up and give him three loaves of bread. Jesus said, "... because of his persistence he will get up and give him whatever he needs."

Persistence in prayer is necessary.

The word "persistence" means repeated requests. The details are incidental. Jesus does not compare God to an unwilling neighbor. The point is clear: If perseverance causes a reluctant neighbor to comply with the wishes of another, how much more God is willing to hear our prayers. The neighbor got up because he didn't want to be bothered anymore. God answers prayer out of pure, paternal love for His children.

How many of us give up on prayer? Persistence does not mean prayer on demand like a promissory note that seals a bargain, nor does it mean our praying is to be a kind of beating upon God's door as if He doesn't hear. Persistence in prayer means wrestling with doubts and fears and taking them all for a talk with God.

Remember how Jacob wrestled the angel in the book of Genesis (ch. 32)? At first Jacob's prayer was self-centered: "Deliver me, please, from the hand of my brother, from the hand of Esau, for I am afraid of him; he may come and kill us all...." Jacob wrestled with the angel all night and said, "I will not let you go, unless you bless me." And the angel asked his name. Jacob complied. The angel said, "You shall no longer be called Jacob, but Israel, for you have striven with God and with humans, and have prevailed."

Do your prayers bring answers like that? Do you ever give up on God? Jesus told the disciples in Luke 24:49, "I am sending upon you what my Father promised; so stay here in the city until you have been clothed with power from on high." The disciples stayed in the city. Finally, they were blessed with the presence of the Holy Spirit.

Jesus Himself struggled in prayer at the Mount of Olives, "In his anguish, he prayed more earnestly, and his sweat became like great drops of blood falling down on the ground" (Luke 22:44). Do your prayers indicate that kind of struggle? Saint Paul urged in 1 Thessalonians (5:17), "... pray without ceasing...."

Bitterness can turn us away from God. Disappointments can turn us away from God. A feeling of hopelessness can turn us away from God. But, cannot God change people? Cannot God change events?

Jesus calmed the winds and the waves. He healed the sick. Christ made the blind see and the cripple walk. He brought the dead back to life.

Cannot He do the same with you? What wave of life should turn you from God? What discouragement should discourage earnest conversation with the Father? Prayer can change people. We don't have to understand spiritual power in order to use it. We do not have to comprehend nuclear energy to see its power. Humans demand too much if prayer is curtailed because of a lack of understanding God's great power.

If God keeps answering "no" to your prayer, you must be asking for favors instead of faith. If you keep on praying rightfully, He will answer "yes" to your prayers. The object of prayer is not to see what we can get out of God but to come into God's very presence. To pray is to know God.

People can erroneously think about prayer. "God, if you will make me well, I will believe in you." "I will go to church, God, if you take away my mental anguish." "I will serve you, God, if you make this come to pass." This pattern of praying is bargaining. It doesn't work.

Our young sons stood in line to see Santa Claus one winter day. Along the way, their parents prompted them to remember what to say when Santa Claus lifted them on his knee. Suffice it to say, prayer is not talking to a Santa Claus.

Prayer lifts us into the very presence of God. If you came into a room and suddenly Jesus walked in and put a hand on your shoulder, would you blurt out a number of requests? No, I think you would fall on your knees and say with Peter, "Lord, be merciful to me a sinner." Prayer is falling on your knees and asking for God's mercy. Persistence, struggle in prayer, strips away puny petitions.

In prayer, the high purposes of God are revealed.

It is significant that this parable follows The Lord's Prayer. Could it be Jesus was saying a model prayer is not enough? Jesus said no father would give a child a serpent if he asked for a fish or would he give a child a scorpion if he asked for an egg. Jesus said, "If you then, who are evil, know how to give good gifts to your children, how much more will the heavenly Father give the Holy Spirit to those who ask him!" (v. 13).

A father can give a son what he needs without any response from the son. But, a father cannot give himself, cannot give his love without the son's willingness to receive it.

God the Father has given His children the blessings of the earth. But, God cannot give the greatest blessing — the Holy Spirit — without receptive hearts. Those who are ready and eager to receive the Holy Spirit receive God in their lives. That is why Jesus can say so certainly, "Ask, and it shall be given you; search, and you will find; knock, and the door will be opened for you" (v. 9).

You are on the wrong track if you endeavor to clarify in your own mind what you would like to do. You have not asked God but consulted your own opinion. You have not sought God but sought your own desires. You have not knocked except on your own brain.

The Holy Spirit is the answer to prayer.

We see what God sees by the Holy Spirit. The Holy Spirit tells us what God has to say. We are not heard for our many words. "When you are praying, do not heap up empty phrases as the Gentiles do; for they think that they will be heard because of their many words" (Matthew 6:7).

It is true that "… your Father knows what you need before you ask him" (Matthew 6:8). The real question is: do you know what you need? Prayer answers that question. Prayer helps us perceive the high purposes of God.

Humility is sorely needed when praying. Humility can reveal His majesty, His loftiness, His goodness and mercy. No perfunctory request for forgiveness will suffice. No get-well quick demand of God will suffice. As George Buttrick said in his book about prayer, "Our prayer must be free of insincerity and the trivial spirit before heaven's beauty is unlocked."

Jesus said to **ask**, to **seek**, and to **knock**. It is necessary to ask directions when visiting a friend. You must learn the friend's address. You must knock on the door when you arrive. You cannot sit outside in your auto at the curb and expect your friend to know you have arrived.

The beautiful part about prayer is that **God is always home**! God does not sit behind locked doors, somewhere beyond the moon. God is as close to us as our breath. God is as close to you as you are to yourself. That door to prayer is always unlocked. The key was thrown away at Calvary. God's address is known. Christ lives!

Beware of setting an alarm clock with your prayer or putting a time limit on God's answer. Beware of half measures in prayer. Be persistent. See the high purpose of God for your life. Receive the Holy Spirit. Our Lord is not only a friend at midnight; He is our Savior!

Sermon 7

Parable of the Rich Farmer

Text: Luke 12:13-21

The parable of the rich farmer is Christ's answer to a rude inquirer. Having just preached to the multitude on acknowledging the "Son of Man" and on the teaching of the Holy Spirit, a man in the multitude blurted out a request, "Teacher, tell my brother to divide the family inheritance with me."

What parent does not know how Jesus felt? In a serious talk with a child, the child trying to remember what he would like to ask the parent, hurriedly changes the subject not hearing the parent at all!

A preacher knows how Jesus felt. His words never reached the man. The hearer was too occupied in thinking of an inheritance that he failed to hear what Christ said. The man wasn't interested in the "Son of Man." He wasn't interested in the consequences of blasphemy. He didn't want to hear about the Holy Spirit. What he was interested in was how to get some cash from his brother.

The interrupter said "Teacher." Christ replied as coldly, "Friend, who set me to be a judge or arbitrator over you?"

The Eastern custom, in the joint family plan, was that the oldest brother administer the patrimony for the family. Two thirds of the estate went to the oldest and one third to the younger. Simply for desire of possessions, the true motive of the interrupter was to change the custom.

Christ did not come to sit on a bench and hand down judicial acts. Christ did not come as a property settler. Rabbis often sat in on judgment and played the role of court. But Jesus was not simply a "teacher." He was God. In talking with God you do not try to use Him. In talking with God you do not register complaints.

We are in the role of a confessor and not complainer when we are talking with God. We cannot exchange complaints for a cross.

What was the trouble with the interrupter? He was covetous. Jesus could have quoted the last two commandments including, "Thou shalt not covet...." He chose to tell a parable.

The parable tells of a rich farmer who determined to keep what he had so he could "eat, drink, be merry," and he died before he could enjoy any of it. What a tragic ending. We learn from this parable that:

Possessions can breed anxiety.

The rich farmer "... thought to himself, 'What should I do, for I have no place to store my crops?' "

The struggle to keep what you have is often as great a struggle as accumulating it in the first place. Many of us have come to know individuals who are so afraid they will lose what they have that they have become insecure.

This rich farmer was consumed with the thought of saving what he had made. There is nothing wrong in thrift. Our Lord had the disciples pick up the baskets of food after feeding the thousands, so that nothing be lost. But if possessions possess you, then that painful uneasiness of mind takes over. Jesus said, "... Do not worry about your life...." If you get too close to your possessions you lose perspective. If you become more interested in possessions than God, then the horizon of Christian living is hidden.

The favorite story of Sigmund Freud, the so-called father of psychiatry, was about a sailor who was shipwrecked on one of the South Sea Islands. The natives lifted him to their shoulders and marched triumphantly into their village. The sailor doubtless thought he was to be their main dish for dinner that night! But, to his astonishment, they put him on a throne, put a crown on his head, and proclaimed him as their king.

He was absolute ruler. Every native was his servant. He enjoyed his new stature in life, but after awhile he began to wonder about it all. He discreetly asked some questions, and he discovered it was their custom once each year to make some man a king, king for a year. He also learned that at the end of the year, the king was banished to an island where he starved to death!

The sailor didn't like that prospect! Being a reasonable fellow, he put his mind to work and he hit upon a marvelous solution. Because he was king, his orders were obeyed. So, he put the natives to building boats. When they had enough boats, he started transplanting fruit trees to the island where he was to be sent. He ordered carpenters to go there and build comfortable houses. He ordered the farmers to clear the land and to plant crops. So, when his kingship was over, he had a place of abundance" (described by Charles L. Allen, *When the Heart Is Hungry*, pp. 108-109).

The other kings had enjoyed life to the fullest. This sailor was foresighted. It is true that we can become so absorbed in tearing down barns and building bigger ones, enjoying what we have, and fail to prepare the journey to another land. Jesus said, "You fool! This very night your life is being demanded of you" (v. 20).

Worry, anxiety, can make us blind. The person whose breakfast is spoiled by what he or she reads in the stock market is in that category. Enjoying life without thought of eternity can make us blind. Christ called the rich farmer a fool because he trusted in possessions.

Possessions can breed arrogance.

Count them! Out of the 61 words spoken by the farmer, twelve refer to himself. "My grain." "My goods." "My soul" he declares!

In what sense were they his? Does not God provide the earth, the soil by which the crops grow?! Does not God send the sunshine and the rain?!

And, what person is independent of others? The farmer didn't tear down those barns and build bigger ones all by himself! The farmer did not plant and harvest the crops alone. The self-made person has yet to be born. Only Christ can make that statement!

Furthermore, Christ did not indiscriminately condemn wealth; he condemned arrogance, a sense of superiority.

The centurion who had slaves and soldiers at his command was praised for his faith in Matthew 7:9. The home of Mary, Martha, and Lazarus was enjoyed by Jesus. Even the soldiers gambled for the robe of Christ so it must have been worth something!

Did you hear about the preacher who once preached on the subject, "What I would do with a million dollars"? After worship, a man came up and handed him a check for that amount. I always wanted to preach that powerful a sermon and get such a reaction! In less than sixty seconds I could tell such a giver what could be done by the church in saving souls!

But, you see, this rich farmer didn't have a sense of stewardship. If you asked him if he believed in God, very likely he would answer in the affirmative. But, if you asked him if he felt he needed God, he might hesitate a bit!

This farmer didn't need God. He didn't seem to give a second thought about his neighbors. He kept everything he had to himself so that he could eat, drink, and be merry. That's why Christ called him a fool. The psalmist chanted it long ago, "Fools say in their hearts, 'There is no God' " (Psalm 14:1). This farmer wasn't lazy. He wasn't greedy. He was just plain arrogant — he lived without God!

Thus, Rudyard Kipling's words describe his complacent doom: "And because we know we have breath in our mouth and think we have thought in our head, we shall assume that we are alive, whereas we are really dead... The lamp of our youth will be utterly out, but we shall subsist on the smell of it, and whatever we do, we shall fold our hands and suck our gums and think well of it. Yes, we shall be perfectly pleased with our work, and that is the perfectest Hell of it" (Rudyard Kipling, *The Old Men*).

Possessed by God is to be rich.

What is wealth? Jesus knew. In John 4:34 He said, "My food is to do the will of him who sent me and to complete his work."

Paul knew what wealth is: "Although I am the very least of all the saints, this grace was given to me to bring to the Gentiles the news of the boundless riches of Christ, and to make everyone see what is the plan of the mystery hidden for ages in God who created all things; so that through the church the wisdom of God in its rich variety might now be made known to the rulers and authorities in the heavenly places" (Ephesians 3:8-10).

The Israelites knew what wealth is: "… remember the Lord your God, for it is he who gives you power to get wealth, so that he may confirm his covenant that he swore to your ancestors, as he is doing today" (Deuteronomy 8:18).

We are possessed by God. "I believe that I cannot by my own reason or strength believe in Jesus Christ my Lord, or come to him; but the Holy Spirit has called me through the gospel, enlightened me by his gifts, and sanctified and preserved me in the true faith; in like manner as he calls, gathers, enlightens, and sanctifies the whole Christian church on earth, and preserves it in union with Jesus Christ in the true faith…." (Luther's answer to the third article of the Apostles' Creed).

To be rich is to accept God-given faith in Christ; to know that when you put your head down on the pillow that everything is right between God and you; to be sure of the forgiveness of sin; to be confident of a greater life "saved in hope," and to know Christ is with you in every phase of life.

The interrupter came to Jesus with an ethical problem on a superficial level. We often do that because we have not solved the deeper question. Because he was covetous, he was in trouble with his brother.

Jesus is saying to any individual that it is not possible to achieve security by amassing property. Covetness is foolish because it tells a lie — the lie that life consists in the abundance of possessions.

For the Christian this is wealth: "And this is eternal life, that they may know you, the only true God, and Jesus Christ whom you have sent" (John 17:3).

Sermon 8

Parable of the Two Builders

Text: Matthew 7:24-27

The parable of the two builders is the conclusion of the Sermon on the Mount, the climax to the greatest sermon ever preached. Listen to your Lord: "And everyone who hears these words of mine and does not act on them will be like a foolish man who built his house on sand. The rain fell, and the floods came, and the winds blew and beat against that house, and it fell — and great was its fall!"

Sense the urgency in Jesus' preaching. "Not everyone who says to me, 'Lord, Lord,' will enter the kingdom of heaven, but only the one who does the will of my Father in heaven" (Matthew 7:21).

"Hearing" and "acting" are keys words of Christ. Hearing the plea of our Lord needs to stir our feelings, stimulate our thinking, and inspire us to action. "Everyone then who hears these words of mine and acts on them will be like a wise man who built his house on rock." In essence, our lives are like building a house.

The parable describes two builders. This is what the parable tells me.

Select with care where and how you build.

Jesus spoke of two men, one wise and the other foolish. The wise built on rock; the foolish built on sand. A person could build on either terrain in Palestine. Jesus spoke in language his hearers understood.

In Palestine, there were wide, dry riverbeds, made by the melting snow from the mountains. Rarely would the snow be so heavy as to be dangerous when melted. It might occur in a generation. Most of the time a little stream trickled down the middle of the wide bed. The person who chose to build there would find it easy to do so. Materials would be close at hand and construction could go fast. A house near a stream meant convenience. A house built on such a site would be sheltered from the winds. It would take less fuel. It was easily accessible. Why shouldn't a person build there?!

To build on rock was difficult. Grading would be necessary on the side of a hill. It would be burdensome to carry the building materials. Once the house was built, it would involve more difficult living. Water would be at some distance. More fuel would be required. Winds would whip around. Why should a person build there?

Which will you do? Built your life on sand or rock? Build your life on your own notion or on God's word?

It isn't easy to be a Christian. That's what this Sermon on the Mount is about. "Blessed are the pure in heart, for they shall see God." "Unless your righteousness exceeds that of the scribes and Pharisees, you will never enter the kingdom of heaven." "… if anyone strikes you on the cheek, turn to him the other also." "Love your enemies and pray for those who persecute you…." "You cannot serve God and mammon…."

The truth of the matter is you cannot embrace the Sermon on the Mount without believing in its author, Jesus Christ. Unless you build your life on Calvary, you build on inclinations and desires that change with the wind; you build on transitory aims beat by the eternal truth of the Creator, "God was in Christ reconciling the world to Himself" (2 Corinthians 5:19).

Yes, it is easier to build life on personal notions, easier to drift along, easier to compromise on life's principles. It is easier to build on sand. Halford Luccock in his *Studies in the Parables of Jesus* wrote "Every duty we omit obscures some truth we might have known" (p. 32).

So, Jesus warns us about where we choose to build, "… And great was the fall of it."

Where will you build? On the sand of self or on the Savior? On the rock of Calvary or on the river of ease? Where you build makes a difference!

Erect a life structure with the scriptures and the sacraments.

What we build is the question. One storm tries both structures.

It is no longer a secret that impressions, thoughts, and volitions gather into a unity. Our days may appear to be haphazard but all of the prime forces frame a personality. Psychologists have argued what is important: emotion, intelligence, or will. There is no mistake that all three are needed. The sermon of Jesus touches on all three. We are to hear and act.

Why are we such self-made authorities on life? Why does a person search for "better ways of living" when the scriptures are so clear? Wasn't it Mark Twain who confessed that it was the parts in the Bible he understood that gave him trouble rather than the parts he did not understand?!

What are you building with? Earnestness alone is not enough. Good intentions alone do not make the real stuff of life. Scripture heard and pondered and lived gives the Holy Spirit material to build your life.

Friendship cannot be built with selfishness. Marriage cannot be built with physical attraction alone. A congregation cannot be built with tradition alone.

Life is a whole with definite character. The house must have a plan. We cannot live from hand to mouth, acting on emotion without intelligence and will. We cannot live on reason alone without the intelligence of God. We cannot live on our own will oblivious to the will of God.

To build on sand with man-made plans is to build superficially. We can fool ourselves with our own wisdom. Wrong won't stand. There is a testing time. When the storm has passed will your structure of life still be there? With what do you build? Can your life stand the test of eternity?

Our Lord is wise. He has given us the word and the sacraments. Without these life cannot stand. Moral structures alone collapse. God-made structures last.

Let the storm come!

When the storm comes, what a person is is revealed. Like coral insects, we live in what we build.

69

Each person is building. Christ's parable is plain. No business person would build a house on sand. Practical people know that sand looks firm and golden in the summer's sun but any thinking person will take into account the winter storms that come with regularity.

The Christian embraces God's truth for his life. The life of the Christian, built on Calvary, is a picture of strength and stability. It will not go to pieces when the storm comes. It will not break down. It will not try to run away.

When the storm of death appears, there is no fear or bitterness. There is no question about the goodness or mercy of God. The Christian is not afraid of death for his loved ones nor is he afraid to die!

Floods will not sweep away faith. Storms will not obstruct vision of the Savior. Rain will not ruin the structure of life. Wind will not cause the Christian to waver.

So, we can say with Tennyson (In Memoriam):

"O living will that shall endure
When all that seems shall suffer shock,
Rise in the spiritual rock,
Flow through our deeds and make them pure."

Friend, build your life on the truth of Calvary. The cross stands "o'er the wrecks of time." The Holy Spirit will help you build life right with scripture and sacrament. Let the storm come! Christ is the same yesterday, today and forever. And, great is the faith that hears and fulfills the word of God. Such a life will stand for eternity!

Sermon 9

Parable of the House that Was Swept Clean and Left Empty

Text: Matthew 12:43-45 see also Luke 11:24-26

When the unclean spirit has gone out of a person, it wanders through waterless regions looking for a resting place, but it finds none. Then it says, "I will return to my house from which I came." When it comes, it finds it empty, swept, and put in order. Then it goes and brings along seven other spirits more evil than itself, and they enter and live there, and the last state of that person is worse than the first. So will it be also with this evil generation.

Our Lord's parable of the house that was swept clean and left empty is a description of humankind's struggle to banish evil.

A few years ago at the crest of the Allegheny Mountains in Pennsylvania, the Sunshine Special stopped to uncouple an engine. Suddenly, a Pullman car broke loose and hurtled down the hill. For three and a half miles the passengers had a common experience, a democracy of terror and an utter nightmare of fright. Finally, the pullman car jumped the track and buried itself in the mountainside. Writes Edwin Poteat, "In Christ, God enters the world's agony and breaks down its downward dash and transmutes it into victory" (reported by Ralph Lowe in his book *The Church and the Amateur*, p. 64).

This parable deals with humankind's downward dash.

Belief in demons was widespread in Jesus' day. Many illnesses were attributed to demon-possession. On occasion, the disciples had not only to deal with demons but with those who claimed to be able to drive away demons. For example, in Mark 9:38-39 John said to Jesus: "... Teacher, we saw someone casting out demons in your name, and we tried to stop him, because he was not following us. But Jesus said, 'Do not stop him; for no one who does a deed of power in my name, will be able soon afterward to speak evil of me.' "

Christ replied to a crowd another time: "Now if I cast out the demons by Beelzubul, by whom do your exorcists cast them out?... But if it is by the finger of God that I cast out the demons, then the kingdom of God has come upon you" (Luke 11:19-20).

Jewish folklore encouraged people to believe demons liked water. Evil spirits dwelt in deserted places, according to Isaiah: "But the wild animals will lie down there, and its houses will be full of howling creatures; there ostriches will live, and there goat-demons will dance" (Isaiah 13:21). Isaiah sounds like a modern double feature *The Return of the Fly* and the *Alligator People* which children cherish to see!

Jesus' teaching is amazing since He used their superstitions to illustrate their plight! In this story of the unclean spirit the demon had been driven out of a person. The demon traveled some distance seeking rest and did not find it in a waterless place. The demon said, "I will return to my house..." No other tenant had replaced him. He entered the house, swept it, and got it in order. He brought seven other demons to live with him fearing his tenancy would be disputed. With these reinforcements he could defy any new attempt to dispossess him. And Jesus said, "... the last state of that person is worse than the first."

It takes courage to sweep evil out.

The house in the parable is a person's soul. Give the person credit. He saw his downward dash. He recognized evil. He faced the evil in his life. He tried to banish it. That takes courage. We never acquire courage by pretense. Evil is in our lives whether we admit it or not. We never gain power over weakness and wrongs until we face them. To have that kind of courage means we must not only be willing to give up our sins, which haunt our hearts and minds, but we must do whatever is required to rid ourselves of them. Fetch the broom and go to work! Sweep sins out of your life.

Delaying tactics do not solve our soul's condition. The mind thrives on such a decision. Our minds can be the biggest deceivers in the world. The mind will trick us. It tries to have you believe that certain things are not really wrong. It will attempt to convince you that you are naturally weak and prompt you to decide there is nothing you can do about it. The mind will try to hide sin in every cranny of its cranium!

Gerald Kennedy in *Who Speaks for God?* states that "the enslaving power of the pleasant habit begins to take hold... throws out a warning now and then, but... ignores the signs and goes on until he cannot break the habit. He believes that somehow the damage that has happened to others cannot happen to him, and the destruction that this behavior has brought to others... assumes will bypass him. Men are not destroyed, as a rule, not because a mighty crisis shatters them into the dust. They are destroyed by a number of small habits which, when added all together spell inefficiency, tawdriness, weakness, and blundering" (p. 112).

The mind can do this to us. Do you have the courage to give up your sins and sweep them out? God cannot come into your life until you are willing to see the downward dash.

The wisdom to bring good in.

It is not sufficient to renounce evil, to sweep it out, and to make resolutions, however. You invite failure if you stop there. An empty house never remains empty. Rats, spiders, termites enter. We need Christ's wisdom to introduce good and replace evil with good.

Look at some notable examples of emptiness:

The Pharisees cast out gross sins but left humankind's soul empty without any real loyalty and love for God. The Jewish nation destroyed idolatry but disregarded true religion. There was no indwelling of God, no lofty enthusiasm, only a set of laws that made the imperfectness of human beings more imperfect.

Wars in our age have been fought to preserve democracy. We destroyed Kaiserism. Hitlerism entered. We destroyed Hitlerism. Communism entered. We destroyed communism. Terrorism entered. And, the last state of the world became worse than the first.

George Buttrick warned us that "nature abhors a vacuum. Life demands its mastery" (*The Parables of Jesus*, p. 76). The soul of human beings is never empty. Every person has some occupant. A demon possesses a soul who invites no worthier tenant.

Whatever occupies your soul is your master. Some are mastered by their bodies. Some are captivated by hard circumstances. Some boast of their freedom and yet are controlled by any whim. The person who does what he likes when he likes is a slave to his likes. Saint Paul claimed to be a slave of Christ!

You cannot leave a house or a soul empty and expect it to remain empty. Something or someone takes over. Harried by our sins, we seek amendment of life and try to sweep away hurtful and harmful life but finally abandon the good life because we cannot do it without God. It takes a cross!

Demons keep their distance when Jesus Christ dwells within. Let Christ come into your life! "Behold, I stand at the door and knock." Let good enter. Read the scriptures. Become an active propagator and participant of the good life in Christ and His church. Sweep out pettiness. Leave the pew and push a few doorbells! Drive out demons. Drive yourself to the cross and on bended knee ask God to bring good into your life. The last state of that person will be better than the first!

The power to keep evil out and the good in.

The problem is to not only to sweep evil out of our lives but to know how to keep it out. The alcoholic could testify to this. The problem of the alcoholic is to keep alcohol out of the body. The alcoholic cannot afford repossession of this disease. It takes more than a broom to sweep away a bottle. We need God's power to keep evil out and the good in.

There is the story of the lady who rented a Jeep to do some heavy work. She went to the beach to get some sand and the Jeep became mired in the sand. The more she tried to get the Jeep out the deeper the rear wheels sank into the sand. Seeking the aid of a garage man, she explained her plight. The garage man told her she did not need a wrecker to get her Jeep out of the sand. But she insisted and at the scene of the difficulty the garage man showed her what to do. The Jeep had a pulling gear and it pulled her right out. The garage man remarked, "That lady thought she was stuck, but she had more power than she realized. She just wasn't using it" (Related by Charles Allen *When the Heart Is Hungry*, p. 154).

In Christian language, faith is the pulling gear. God's great gift of faith bestowed upon a believer is the right gear. If you are stuck in the sand of Satan, God can pull you out. If you are on a downward dash, God can break your crashing speed and translate life into victory.

Would you like to overcome some evil spirit and sinful habit? Beware then of eliminating spiritual values. Let Christ rule. His yoke is easy. His victory on the cross is the assurance that believers will dwell in the house of the Lord forever.

Sermon 10

Parable of the Last Judgment

Text: Matthew 25:31-46

The parable of the last judgment describes a person's central life attachment, the basis on which life is finally judged.

The words of Jesus were well remembered, containing elements of magnificent Hebrew poetry, expressing the heart of religion as Jewish Christians came to understand it. He explains the basis of the last judgment, spoken three days before His own judgment by humankind.

Christ will judge.

The parable begins with the words: "When the Son of man comes in His glory, and all the angels with Him, then He will sit on His glorious throne. Before Him will be gathered all the nations, and He will separate people one from another as a shepherd separates the sheep from the goats."

Christ will return. All humankind will kneel before Him. Every person must appear. No one will be exempt. Every different face and life that ever existed will be brought before Jesus.

Do you believe this? It will make a difference if you believe that Christ will return and judge your life.

Crime is all around us. If criminals knew they would be caught, would they have committed the crime? Criminals know when they are breaking the law.

In another sense, closer to our conscience: Are your automobile driving habits any different when a patrolman is in sight?! Have you ever seen a speeding car go around a motorcycle policeman?! I have not. Everyone is careful to observe the speed limit when a policeman is seen. Car drivers make a mental check whether in the correct lane and peek at the speedometer! Sometimes a long line of cars results when following a police car. No one dares go around! But, the second the police car disappears down some ramp, the line of cars quickly disappear!

Some believe they will not be caught in committing a crime. Some think they can exceed the speed limit as long as they keep their eye on the rearview mirror. Some refuse to believe there will be a judgment day. The convicted criminal can tell you he was caught. The speeding motorist brought to a screeching halt by a siren tells you he was caught. The Christian brought to the feet of Jesus, in penitent confession, can warn: "Do not be deceived; God is not mocked, for whatever a man sows, that he will also reap" (Galatians 6:7).

There is the story of a man who visited an art gallery. When he looked at the work of the great masters, he said to the attendant, "I don't think the pictures are so good." The attendant replied, "Excuse me, sir, the pictures are not on trial."

So, we do not judge. Someone has written a little jingle:

"There is so much good in the worst of us,
And so much bad in the best of us,
That it hardly becomes any of us
To talk about the rest of us."

I need to remember that jingle!

Christ will judge. All nations, all peoples, all races will be brought before Him. He will judge every person fairly. He will be able to separate the righteous from the unrighteous as easily as a Palestinian shepherd can separate the white Syrian sheep from the black Syrian sheep, at dusk! There will be no shadow of doubt on judgment day!

The criterion of Christ's judgment.

On what basis will Christ judge? What is the dividing line? Jesus did not say we would be judged by our nationality, our social status, our race, or by any accident of earthly rank.

Jesus did not say a person would be honored because he gave a cup of water to a thirsty vagrant or wrote out a million dollar check.

Jesus stated clearly that a person will be judged on his main attachment in life. Those who put God at the center of life have conscience and compassion. Those who serve "idols" revel in money, leisure, fashion, and flesh.

Jesus mentioned unaffected kindness: feeding the poor, being hospitable to the stranger, clothing the naked, visiting the sick, sharing loneliness with the prisoner. These traits cited by our Lord are not shallow acts. Occasional displays of philanthropy cannot be substituted for faith.

We are judged by our controlling motives. "The good person brings good things out of a good treasure, and the evil person brings evil things out of an evil treasure. I tell you, on the day of judgment you will have to give an account for every careless word you utter..." (Matthew 12:35-37).

Good works spring from faith. Philanthropic works can spring from pride. Unaffected kindness is sincere and loves because God is love. Self-righteousness gazes at God, beats upon his breast, and is thankful he is not like other folks.

On the basis of Christ's judgment, does righteous living spring from your life? Do you love people for God's sake? What have you done to spread the gospel throughout the world? Is that unused garment hanging in your closet being withheld from the needy? Is that almighty dollar in your pocket stuck fast to your selfish self? When were you sympathetic with the uncomfortable, loving the unlovely?

We all come under God's judgment. The centrality of attachment in life determines the direction of life. We are judged by our sincerity and by our controlling motives.

We need to see God's identification with human beings. This parable begins with these words: "When the Son of Man comes...." It is the Son of Man who shows us the meaning of kindness, who gives us hope of eternal life, who makes sense out of the golden rule, who shows us the motive of love. "The true light that enlightens every man was coming into the world; he was in the world, and the world was made through him, yet the world knew him not. But to all who receive him, who believe in his name, he gave power to become the children of God; who were born, not of blood nor of the will of the flesh nor of the will of man, but of God" (John 1:9-13).

There is love, kindness, and our controlling motive. There is God in Christ reconciling us to Him. This is the criterion of Christ's judgment: "But to all who receive him, who believed in his name, he gave power to become children of God" (John 1:12).

Are you a child of God? One of His sheep?

Surprises in Christ's judgment.

There will be some surprises on judgment day. In the parable Jesus has the righteous exclaiming: "Lord, when was it that we saw you hungry and gave you food, or thirsty and gave you something to drink? And when was it that we saw you a stranger and welcomed you, or naked and gave you clothing? And when was it that we saw you sick or in prison and visited you?"

The righteous were unaware of their deeds for Christ. Since Jesus identified Himself with human need, their deeds were also for Christ. They did good without thought of reward. They served others because they loved the Son of Man. They had charity, for their stem of life was rooted in Christ. They were Christlike because Christ was in them. They were godly because God's power guided them.

The unrighteous were unaware of God's presence in everyday life. "Lord, when was it that we saw you hungry or thirsty or a stranger or naked or sick or in prison, and did not take care of you?"

Aha! If they had only known! If they had seen Christ, not incognito, they would have rushed to His side. They surmised that the way to get ahead is to cultivate the good graces of important people. They said within themselves: "It doesn't matter who you know but who knows you!"

Sales talks do not result in righteousness. Spiritual pep talks on peace of mind and pathways to happiness do not produce spirituality in a person.

Notice Jesus did not lay crimes at the feet of the unrighteous. No one was charged with the big sins. They were simply respectable, decent people who didn't do anybody any good. They were introspective, caring for their own, despising the brotherhood and sisterhood of the world. They quenched the fountain of love.

Real love is life. Lovelessness is its own demon. The lawyer in Luke 10, desiring to demonstrate his righteousness, asked

Jesus the identity of his neighbor. The answer was: "Go and do likewise."

Christ will judge. He has the last word. You and I will be judged on our main attachment in life. The question is: Is God your source of love? Is God the basis of your life? Is Christ the power and the motive?

Judgment day will bring some surprises. What kind of surprise is in store for you?

Sermon 11

Christ at the Bier

Text: Luke 7:11-16

The day was dark and dreary for a number of people in the city of Nain. One of their young men had just died. He was the only son of a widow. The crowd of mourners, with the mother, had begun the procession down the hill outside the city gate toward the cemetery.

Another procession was moving up the hill ready to enter the city of Nain at the main gate. Christ and His disciples headed that procession. A great crowd of people had followed them. They had heard of Jesus' parable of the two houses. They had witnessed the healing of the centurion's slave, the miracle performed from a distance.

These two processions meet, one headed for the burial ground, the other headed for the city. It is a dramatic meeting of life and death.

I had occasion to witness a funeral procession on one of my evangelism missions in Puerto Rico. As in Jesus' time, in Puerto Rico, burial occurs within a few hours after death. This procession on foot was led by two girls carrying flowers. The immediate family and friends followed the casket rolled by pallbearers down the dusty street. When they reached the church, a priest emerged and in a few seconds pronounced a blessing. The procession quickly continued to the cemetery outside the city gates. I learned that the dead man was poor. They told me if he had been wealthy, the casket would have been taken inside the church for the blessing. How cold and heartless it seemed. The entire scene lacked compassion.

My thoughts turned to Nain. Jesus had seen a similar procession. In contrast, Jesus had compassion.

81

The mother was grieving since she had lost her husband; now she had lost her only child. Walking unsteadily, she was hardly aware of the crowd with her on its way to the grave. She did not expect or anticipate anything happening. She had been to the burial ground before. She knew by past experience what it meant to bury a loved one.

Christ was quick to size up the situation. He had compassion.

We are not always ready to see the significance of such processions. We can be so absorbed with ourselves that we might not even notice a funeral procession. People can become hard and insensitive to the cold facts of death and its emotional strain in the bereaved hearts. I always notice the workmen at a cemetery. A man may be mowing lawn but as soon as a funeral procession approaches, he stops his tractor and bares his head in respect for the dead and the mourners.

Jesus could have ignored the procession to the gravesite with a crowd following Him. He stopped His own procession. Christ is free from selfishness. He felt the mother's pain and sorrow.

This is the God we worship! The children of Israel had melted precious possessions in molding a golden idol. An idol could show no compassion. The idols of fame and fortune cannot say, "Do not weep." We worship the God of the heart and worship the God who has a feeling for people.

It would not matter how much compassion Christ had or how tenderly he pitied if He is only a historical figure who displayed perfect manners in a given situation, and who had the uncanny ability for showmanship. People can do nice things for others in bereavement, but can they act? God dries tears before raising the dead. He gives assurance of His sympathy. He encourages expectation. He pledges to do what is necessary. Christ had compassion.

A bishop was stopped by a woman outside the church with a request. Her husband was drunk down the street a short way. Everybody in the community knew he was a drunk. She wanted the bishop to help her put her husband in the car so she could take him home. The woman loved her husband although he was a drunk.

The bishop was in a hurry. The worship celebration was about to begin. He told the woman that he was sorry but he was late already and must go inside. The bishop began the worship robed in clerical garments. Then it dawned on him what he had done. He had refused to help when he was due in church. He had passed by on the other side. Turning to the congregation he said, "Please sing another hymn or two. There is something I must do. I will be right back." The bishop then dashed out of the church with his robes flowing and helped the lady put her husband into the car!

It is a lesson for all of us. Christ was never too occupied to help people. He stopped His own procession when He saw this mother. No evidence of faith was displayed. There was no prayer by the mother. If God always waited until a person prayed, God's grace would never be known. In the catechism we learn God already knows our need. God feels the necessity of revealing Himself. We are led to desire better gifts in life by the Holy Spirit. God does not suppress natural emotion. In our tears we catch glimpses of the eternal day before us. Christ in His compassion for us encourages us to hope. Expectation never looks backward but looks forward to the procession of God's people to an eternal home.

Christ touched the bier.

The two processions at Nain met that day. Christ stopped the procession by touching the bier. The bearers of the bier stopped. Christ said, "Young man... Rise!"

Only Christ can stop the death march. He stops the pain of death. It was by His own death that He imparted life that "whosoever believeth in Him shall not perish." Christ stops death's forebodings. Christ eliminates eternal damnation.

Christ accomplishes this with His own power. Our Lord did not assume too much on that day in Nain. "The dead man sat up and began to speak, and Jesus gave him to his mother."

Christ touched people on other occasions. He used clay to heal the blind. He used spittle to heal the deaf. Christ Himself had the power.

Christ calmed the winds and called to the dead. The dead hear him. Faith sees that Christ has authority in all realms. If the dead hear him, then people have another life. "Very truly, I tell you, the hour is coming, and is now here, when the dead will hear the voice of the Son of God, and those who hear will live" (John 5:25).

"The dead man sat up and began to speak...." I wonder what the young man said. What a testimony he could give. He was dead but now is alive. The father of the prodigal son rejoiced in the rebirth of his wayward son and the mother of the young man at Nain rejoiced in the new birth of her only son.

In the hour of death and in the hour of life the world needs the testimony of people who have been touched by the Savior. How many times has God stopped our destructive procession by word and sacrament? What did we say?

Willie Loman, in the play *The Death of a Salesman*, speaks: "The woods are burning, boys, you understand? There's a big blaze going all around."

The idols of skepticism and agnosticism say nothing can stop the fire. The fire must burn itself out. The procession of Nain is an illustration of how our Lord stops the fire. The Christian testifies that God stops the procession of damnation.

> "There was no other good enough
> To pay the price of sin;
> He only could unlock the gate
> Of heaven, and let us in."

Christ gave the young man to his mother.

The purpose of the miracle was not to establish Christ's claims but to give comfort. Mother and son were reunited.

You can catch the joy of this occasion if you have ever attended a family reunion and one of those old-fashioned summertime picnics. That widow never forgot the day Jesus walked into her city. That son never forgot the thrill of living again.

Luke included in his writings Jesus' special and very tender concern for women. "And he gave him to his mother."

The miracle tells us of Christ's compassion. It tells us of Christ's authority. There will be a resurrection day. Dear ones will be given back to empty, outstretched arms. Hungry hearts will be fed in seeing loved ones in the arms of Jesus. Christ will reunite your family.

The boy at Nain was not the last boy Christ will raise. God gave His son. Christ returned. It is because of Jesus' life, death, and resurrection all believers will join hands in the eternal circle of faith.

Fear seized the people where two processions met. They said, "A great prophet has arisen among us!" and "God has visited his people."

Christ still stops processions, destined for the cemetery or destined for destruction. There is hope in Christ. Christ was at the bier in Nain. He is also with us today. "Do not weep... Young man, I say to you, rise!" "The dead man sat up and began to speak...."

Sermon 12

A Lesson on Humility

Text: Luke 14:1-11

Jesus occasionally was invited by religious leaders to dine with them. He never refused. Lawyers and Pharisees were present, Luke records, in the case of Nicodemus' invitation and "… they were watching him closely." An important person can relate how it feels to feast while others watch.

The Jews were extremely careful concerning their ceremonial laws. For example, to have guests for a meal on the sabbath meant the meal had to be prepared the previous day and kept warm. Others could look in on at the feast, since manners in those days permitted. This explains the presence of the man with the dropsy, a disease common in Jerusalem. It can be debated whether the Pharisees baited the trap by inviting the man with the dropsy to view the feast, hoping his presence might prompt Jesus to heal him.

Jesus' action cannot be debated. He asked the Pharisees and scribes a question: "Is it lawful to cure people on the sabbath, or not?" They did not answer. They found his question unanswerable, although their prejudices still existed. Jesus healed the man and sent him away.

Jesus turned His attention and His hearers' attention to another subject, the subject of humility. Noting the guests had made a mad scramble for the best seats, He said, "When you are invited by someone to a marriage banquet, do not sit down at the place of honor, in case someone more distinguished than you has been invited by your host; and the host who invited both of you may come and say to you, 'Give this person your place,' and then in disgrace you would start to take the lowest place. But when you are invited, go and sit down at the lowest place, so that when your host comes he may say to you 'Friend, move up higher'; then you will be honored in the presence of all who sit at the table with you. For all who exalt themselves will be humbled, and those who humble themselves will be exalted."

This parable is not a lesson about proper behavior at a banquet. It penetrates much deeper and measures pride. These words of Jesus are for us as well as for the Pharisees. What shall we say then?

Humility knows gratitude.

View this man in Jesus' parable, striding forward as an invited guest and sitting at a table where all can see him and where he has the best view. Sitting there self-contented, the host tells him his seat is for another guest. He begins to find another place and by this time most of the seats have been taken. Self-consciously, he sinks into a seat far down at the table.

This is a commentary on how we act. Life is set before us as a banquet. Many seek the chief places. The man who believes himself self-made is sitting undeservedly at the head able. Imagine also a person next to him saying to himself, "I deserve everything I have; I earned it."

Pride sits at the head table, aware of himself and unaware of his host.

John Bunyan in *The Shepherd Boys Sing* writes:

"He that is down needs fear no fall,
He that is low, no pride;
He that is humble ever shall
Have God to be his guide."

Dante in Virgil heard voices singing, "Blessed are the poor in Spirit," and noticed that, though he was climbing, progress was easier than it had been on level ground. Whereupon Dante felt his brow, for true humility is unconscious of being humble. (Cited by George Buttrick, *Parables of Jesus*, p. 84).

Therefore, humility is unaware of itself but is aware of God's gifts. God has given so much.

Humility knows reverence.

Knowledge, skill, ambition, the ability to win others' regard have been the resources of our generation. We are beginning to understand they are not sufficient. Life demands sterner and more resilient qualities of life. It is good to have knowledge and skill. We need these to improve the higher standards of living. Ambition is admirable. Enjoying the respect of others gives a certain feeling of belonging. Truman B. Douglas expressed it rightly: "But, what can give us the staying power to outlast circumstances when things do not come out right? When all that is controllable has been controlled, there still are accident, misfortune, the knowledge of finiteness, the loss of loved ones, the prospect of our own death, and always the possibility of awful chaos in man's collective planning and history" (*Why Go to Church?*, p. 117).

Reverence for God has the thrust of trust. That is what humility consists of and is full of hope.

The story was heard first in London, of a young pianist cruelly wounded in the war, gaining consciousness and discovering the loss of his right arm. He languished for months in heartbroken despondency and mental suffering. Finally, with the slow return of health, a friend brought him to Sir Walford Davies, the distinguished composer. Sir Walford took him for a walk across the campus to a cathedral and, upon entering, asked the young man to wait there. Sir Walford went to the organ and played for half an hour. When he returned, the young man looked up almost bitterly and said, "Why do you torture me like this? Once I could play like that." Sir Walford spoke gently, "You can play like that again, young man. For the last half hour I played with my left hand and the pedals." The man who told the story said, "I do wish that you could have been here last evening. You would have heard him play with the London Symphony Orchestra "Ravel's Concerto for the Left Hand" (reported by Ralph Lowe *The Church and the Amateur Adult*, p. 86).

Pride gave the young man no hope. Pride dwelt only on loss. Pride dwells only on self. Humility lifts our eyes to God. Humility has reverence and gives hope.

Humility knows forgiveness.

The lawyers and Pharisees in banquet with Jesus were not conscious of sin. They were conscious of the law. Today some Christians are conscious of the Bible but not conscious of sin forgiven. Not only do we need to be conscious of rebellion against God but conscious of God's forgiveness when we rebel. Pride wants us to believe we do not need forgiveness. A more subtle device of pride is to help us live without the power of the knowledge of sin forgiven.

The Pharisees in their day did not experience God's power because they didn't experience the forgiveness of sin. Adherence to law gave them their only sense of security. Jesus punctured a hole in their concept of religion.

God in Christ reconciled the world!

Three days after Mahatma Gandhi's death, at a mass gathering in India, Srimathi Sarojini Naidu opened her speech with these words: "Master, it is three days since you died. Come back, come back." Daniel Niles said, "That is the hungry cry of the human soul, the cry for living companionship; it is a presence we want, not just principles; a teacher, not just teachings" (*That They May Have Life*, p. 26).

The Christian does not have to plead with Christ to return. He did return. Christ bestows forgiveness. The Christian is humbled by this knowledge. See what God has done! He has prepared a feast for believers. It is our privilege to accept forgiveness with gratitude and reverence. Humility consists of all three: gratitude, reverence, forgiveness!

A dash of humility is good for the soul!

Sermon 13

Take Heart — Sin Forgiven!

Text: Matthew 9:1-8

"And after getting into a boat he crossed the sea and came to his own town. And just then some people were carrying a paralyzed man lying on a bed. When Jesus saw their faith, he said to the paralytic, 'Take heart, son; your sins are forgiven' "

— Matthew 9:1-2

Our Lord performs three miracles following the Sermon on the Mount: the stilling of the storm; the casting out of the demons; and this miracle, the healing of the paralytic.

The most important part of this miracle is the forgiveness of sins. The relationship between Christ's miracles and His ordinary work should encourage the Christian. Towering high above His miracles is His power to forgive sin!

Our deepest need is forgiveness.

Friends brought the paralytic to Jesus with eagerness and earnestness. Jesus saw their faith and said, "Take heart, son; your sins are forgiven." They had come for Christ's healing of the boy. Jesus bypassed the disease for the moment and spoke the great word of pardon. Jesus went straight to the heart of the problem. The palsy was the result of the sufferer's vice, and probably he felt whatever may have been his friends' wishes for him, he needed forgiveness most. This conclusion seems fair since Christ would never have offered forgiveness to an impenitent or indifferent heart.

Amid all our clamor and hungry needs, God's forgiveness is our deepest need.

A person's most important relationship in this world is his relationship with God.

Two young men entered a church to ridicule a priest and said at the altar, "Jesus Christ died for me and I don't care." The priest replied, "But, young men, the point is that Jesus loved you enough to die for you!"

Whether a president or king, professor or laborer, people of culture or people of ignorance, our chief need is forgiveness. Whatever else a wise physician pays little attention to secondary symptoms but grapples with the disease, likewise our Lord dealt with this paralytic. Christ desires to deal with us in the same manner.

Christ's forgiveness is divine.

The Pharisees who criticized Jesus were right. Forgiveness *is* an exclusively divine act. Sin deals only with God. Vice deals with the laws of morality. Crime deals with the laws of the land. The same act may be vice, crime, and sin. It deals with self and others and in the last with God. All come under God's control and sin committed is against God and only God can forgive.

Sin is rebellion against God, a perversion that destroys our relationship with God. Sin's consequences are its penalties and are removed by forgiveness. Pardon is love surrounding the former rejection and entering the heart.

What does it mean when fathers and mothers forgive their children? It means their love is neither deflected nor embittered by their wrongdoing, and love enters their children's heart. God's forgiveness is similar: "Take heart; sin is forgiven!"

Sermon 14

Parable of the Marriage Feast

Text: Matthew 22:1-14

The wedding banquet of a king's son, in Jesus' day, was prepared with lavish hospitality. Invitations were sent many days prior to the event. The king's household spent its time, night and day, planning and executing every detail for the great day. The king spared nothing. This was the day he had anticipated. It would be a memorable day for his son and bride. Marriage in that time and in ours is a joyous occasion. Jesus compares the feast to the kingdom of heaven.

Luther said in reference to this parable: "He calls it a marriage feast, not a time of toil or a time of sorrow, but a time of holiday and a time of joy; in which we make ourselves fine, sing, play, dance, eat, drink, are glad, and have a good time; else it would not be a wedding feast, if people were working, mourning, or crying. Therefore, Christ calls His Christianity and gospel by the name of the highest joy on earth; namely, by the name of a marriage feast."

The Invitations.

The king sent his servants to call those who were invited to the marriage feast, but they refused to come. The invitation was offered again by other servants sent by the king but they ridiculed it and departed, one to his farm, another to his business, and so on.

God's invitation went to the farmer and to the city person. Jesus paints a picture of His generation's unbelief: "They made light of it." They were too busy and paid no attention.

What about the widespread unbelief of our generation, disregarding the cross and the resurrection? Should God's invitation be clearer? Many make light of the invitation. Before the crucifixion, our Lord stood alone before Pilate. No disciples were present to speak in behalf of Jesus. Is Christ before unbelievers of our day and are the saints of the church supporting Him?

America has made God too small. We forbid use of the Bible in education and prayer in our schools. We make light of daily prayer. We fail to use Christian principles in business. We ignore God, content to work out problems in our own time and in our own way.

Is unbelief in our generation in high and low places? If a person becomes excited over a baseball series can he not also become excited about the Savior? A stranger in the street would say, "How about those Yankees? Or how about those Dodgers?" Does the church say, "How about Christ?"

Unbelief? We Americans are the apostles of religious tolerance. We put companionship above conviction. We want to include everyone in a nice democracy where two cars are in every garage and two gods for every home, a god for the nation, and a god for personal use.

Jesus said other servants were sent and were killed. Some rejecters of the invitation were more violent than others. The king became angry. The murderers were destroyed. Rejected love brings wrath. "The God of many nominal Protestants today is incapable of anger. He is nothing more than the magnificent oversized portrait of a sentimental human father who is incapable of the slightest desire to discipline his children," said Walter Barlow (*God so Loved*, p. 53).

Ways of sinning.

The king in Jesus' parable invited the general public. "Those slaves went out into the streets and gathered all whom they found, both good and bad; so the wedding hall was filled with guests." God's offer is to all without discrimination. It is given to the good and the bad. Conclusion: the church is to serve both.

Two ways of sinning are: refusing to accept God's invitation and taking the invitation of God in an outward way and continuing in sin.

The king noticed one guest without a wedding garment. It is impossible for anyone to hide from God in a crowd. The other guests have not noticed the fellow without a wedding garment. The king noticed. He was astonished at the man's rude boldness, knowing that he came without the proper attire.

The wedding garment is God-given righteousness and purity. A nominal Christian says he has accepted God but lives in sin, not putting off the "old man."

Thomas á Kempis in *The Imitation of Christ* said, "Some carry their devotion only in books, some in pictures, some in outward signs and figures. Some have Me often in their mouth; but little of Me in their heart" (p. 28).

The king thought this fellow must have a reason for not wearing a garment. "Friend, how did you get in here without a wedding robe?" He was speechless. He was self-condemned. The king had him bound hand and foot and Jesus said he was thrown "... into the outer darkness, where they will be weeping and gnashing of teeth."

Many are called; few chosen.

Those who choose not to receive God's invitation are not chosen by God although they are called by God.

I have passed through the Panama Canal many times. For example, a ship comes into the Canal from the Atlantic. A gate is in front of the ship. A gate falls behind it. A man in an unseen control room pulls a lever. The ship is lifted noiselessly to a new level. What is the explanation? Through the months the rains have been falling up in the hills. Down through creeks and rivers the waters have flowed into a large reservoir. The Canal is connected to the reservoir. When the lever is pulled, the waters flow under the ship with power sufficient to lift the ship to a higher level for further progress. "This is what happens when Christians are in touch with the illimitable power of God. They are lifted by his power to new levels of thinking and acting for further progress" (described by Jesse M. Bader *Evangelism in a Changing America*, pp. 137-138).

The call of the kingdom is to a higher level of living. Growth in faith takes us from one level to another, from the level of self to the Savior.

Sermon 15

Saint Luke, an Evangelist

Text: 2 Timothy 4:5-11

> Paul speaks: "Do your best to come to me soon, for Demas, in love with this present world, has deserted me and gone to Thessalonica; Crescens has gone to Galatia, Titus to Dalmatia. Only Luke is with me. Get Mark and bring him with you, for he is useful in my ministry."
>
> — 2 Timothy 4:9-11

Days in the church year honor individuals who have served our Lord and His church in a remarkable way. Luke is honored on October 18.

Luke was a physician and companion of Paul. The third gospel and the Acts of the Apostles were written by Luke. Both books describe something of Luke's life.

Luke joined Paul at Troas as a companion on Paul's second missionary journey. Some believe Luke was the man of Macedonia who appealed to Paul for help. Luke rejoined Paul on his third missionary journey. At Philippi during Paul's imprisonment at Caesarea, Luke had opportunity to gather material for his gospel. He is called the "Evangelist" since he is believed to be the author of one of the four gospels. Gospel means "good news," the good news being Christ's life; His victory over evil and death. "Evangelist" means the good news proclaimed by pen and by tongue.

Paul and Luke were companions. Luke, the physician, cared for the physically afflicted Paul. Luke's writings reveal his well-trained mind, his excellent literary ability, his interest in the welfare of people, and his skill in narrating events that would interest a physician. For example: the recording of the birth of John and Jesus, reference to the "great fever" in Luke 4:38, the ability of

Jairus' daughter to eat "meat" after she recovered, the inclusion of the parable of the Good Samaritan with its first aid episode.

"Luke was a kindly, evangelistic literary genius and first-century physician who dedicated all that he had to the universal Christ in varied service to his fellow men" as described in Harper's Dictionary (p. 403).

We consider this text with this background. I owe Alexander Maclaren for his suggestive outline on this passage. Other characters are mentioned in Paul's writing of 2 Timothy.

Demas.

"For Demas, in love with this present world, has deserted me and gone to Thessalonica...."

Paul was in prison and 2 Timothy is his last letter. His martyrdom is near. "I have fought the good fight, I have finished the race, I have kept the faith" (2 Timothy 4:7).

Demas did not keep the faith. This grieved Paul. We know very little of Demas although Paul honored him by the designation "fellow-worker." He had been admitted into that inner circle, was trusted and considered a man of some maturity. History records him of being "in love with this present world." He deserted Paul.

In 1 John 2:15 we read, "Do not love the world or the things in the world. The love of the Father is not in those who love the world; for all that is in the world -- the desire of the flesh, the desire of the eyes, the pride in riches -- comes not from the Father but from the world. And the world and its desires are passing away, but those who do the will of God live forever."

These statements frequently puzzle people. When one views the beauty of the earth and the majesty of the ocean waves, it is not wrong to love this beauty.

Paul said Demas was "in love with this present world." Demas' characteristics often dominate us and Thessalonicas entice us. We are all exposed to the same danger. We are inclined to fall prey to the world's spell and too weak to ward off its intriguing invitations.

Notice the strong appeal of "this present world" and how persistent it is. We are connected with it. You and I have business for tomorrow. Each of us has a task. Our hands and minds are busy with things around us. Our path is difficult, like living on a knife edge.

False asceticism is not proclaimed by Christianity. It is our duty to work, to be occupied with the world, but it is fatal to become enslaved by it. We can appreciate God's creation. But if we become its slave we become like Demas, so occupied, so absorbed in temporal things we fail to reflect the greater good, which is eternal. We are not to be "in love with this present world."

When the love of this old world possesses us, once the lust of it enters our hearts and establishes a footing, it becomes impossible for the love of Christ to be dominate. We cannot have two masters. When our plans and schemes are anchored in the fleeting illusory present, there is no room for the ennobling presence of Jesus Christ.

Have you seen a balloon that the army uses in reconnaissance rise? It will not ascend unless the ropes are loosened. Unless we loosen the ropes of this world our hearts can never enjoy the omnipresence of the living Christ. He will not come into our lives until we allow Him to live within us.

Which two shall we choose? Paul chose the lonely cell. His heart was broken when the companion who previously heard Christ's message ran away to a Thessalonica.

Mark.

"Get Mark and bring him with you, for he is useful in my ministry."

Tragedy and triumph are behind these words. Mark left Paul in Perga on Paul's first missionary journey. We do not know all the circumstances but there was a separation. Barnabas wanted Mark to go with them but Paul refused. Paul took Silas with him and Barnabas took Mark on his journey. Somehow things changed. No doubt Mark relented. Paul forgave. Mark was reinstated in Paul's favor.

Mark ran away, like Demas, but he returned. Barnabas had protected Mark but in his kindness he had been cruel. Paul with indignation had been kinder.

What does Mark's restoration tell us? We cannot travel beyond the forgiving love of Christ no matter how far we have traveled from God. Christ laid down the terms of forgiveness when He said we are to forgive "seventy times seven."

What did the restored runaway receive? Trust. Previously Paul felt it was a mistake to take Mark with him; now he wanted Mark to serve.

Failure teaches us to be successful. Sin weakens. Acknowledged sin coupled with forgiven sin, brings us closer to God. A deeper humility, a deeper gratitude, and an awareness of the weak places in our lives is the result.

Luke.

"Only Luke is with me."

Paul's steadfast companion had been with him for years, having joined him first at Troas, remaining with him at Philippi, and then rejoining him at Philippi on his return journey, and traveling with him to Jerusalem, Caesarea, in a shipwreck, in Rome for his first imprisonment, and then his second imprisonment.

Luke was a steadfast soul who did not stray but with patience and communion with Christ was strengthened. He was an evangelist. God's power served Luke wherever God sent him.

A man shoveling snow experienced a heart attack. A truck driver noticed him on the sidewalk, stopped and rushed him to a hospital. The doctor ripped open his shirt, cut him open, massaged his heart with his hands but could not restore the beat. Then the doctor took an extension cord, stripped the rubber off the wires, plugged the cord into the wall outlet, plunged the wires of the cord into the man's heart and the shock enabled the heart to beat. Because of a doctor's skill and a truck driver's help the man lived.

We need more truck drivers who rescue people and take them to the Great Physician. We need more Lukes who steadfastly help in time of need. The Christian church needs all types of people to walk with Jesus.

Who are you? A Demas headed for Thessalonica? Stop in your tracks and return with Mark. Are you a Luke? Are you ready to serve Jesus anywhere, anytime, anyplace? Or have you run away? You can return and continue "steadfast, immovable, always excelling in the work of the Lord, because you know that in the Lord your labor is not in vain" (1 Corinthians 15:58).

Sermon 16

Luther's Love Life

Text: Romans 3:21-28

"But now, apart from law, the righteousness of God has been disclosed, and is attested by the law and the prophets, the righteousness of God through faith in Jesus Christ for all who believe.... For we hold that a person is justified by faith apart from works prescribed by the law."

— Romans 3:21-22, 28

The book of Romans lay dormant for centuries until a young man of twenty saw for the first time a complete Bible chained in a library. The words which changed this young man's life and also changed the church: "For we hold that a person is justified by faith apart from works...."

Martin Luther was reared in the strict religious atmosphere of the Roman Catholic church but with little knowledge of the Bible. He was terrified by thoughts of God's wrath. The sudden death of a friend intensified these thoughts. Although destined for a legal career and having earned a master's degree, he entered an Augustinian monastery in Erfurt, Germany, at the age of 21. His father was disappointed and grief stricken by his decision. Luther continued his theological training and was ordained to the priesthood. However, his theological studies brought him no inward peace. An old master of studies in the monastery encouraged him to center his hopes on the article of the forgiveness of sins. Vicar of the order, Johann von Staupitz, also instructed him in this article.

Luther's love for the scriptures.

Although Luther lectured at Wittenberg as a professor of philosophy, he turned his attention to the Bible. The decisive change in his life was brought about in studying the Bible and in lecturing on books of the Bible, Romans, Psalms, Galatians, Hebrews, Titus, and Judges.

"For Luther, the Bible was the word of God not because the church said so, but because in its pages he came face-to-face with God. He knew, from that moment, that he needed further assurance God had met with him and spoken to him in the Bible and that was sufficient (A.M. Chirgwin *The Bible in World Evangelism*, pp. 32-33).

The situation created by the Bible may be illustrated from the experience of an English pilot when he told the story of how he was taken prisoner. He was caught in a cone of a searchlight from the ground while flying over enemy territory. No matter which way he turned or what stunts he performed, he could not escape that light. Pastor Harold Albert who told this story, made this application: "This is our task; to hold people in the light of the Word of God, that even though they be uncomfortable, and disturbed in it, they may, nevertheless, be held until won by the love that will not let us go."

That kind of light and love held Luther. That kind of light and love held Saint Paul, "Saul, Saul, why do you persecute me?" (Acts 9:4).

It was that kind of light and love that held Justin, Tatian, and Theophilus, to become Christian. Justin's interests were wholly philosophical since he attended the lectures of many of the best known philosophers of the time. He studied under a stoic, a Pythagorean, and a Platonist. But none of them satisfied him. At last an old man "led him from Plato to the Prophets, from metaphysics to the Gospels (Jackson Foakes, *History of the Christian Church*, p. 158).

God converted the church's first missionary with light and love. God directed the church to His Word by leading an Augustinian monk to the inspired words of that missionary.

The Bible is a book of light and love. Spurgeon spoke of the Bible when asked how he would defend it: "The Bible is like a lion. Let it loose and it will defend itself."

In the church's mission, God's instrument is the Bible. Free the Bible. It was chained in Luther's day but not chained now. Do we know the Bible?

A lady found herself seated next to a bishop at a dinner. Keeping the conversation running along channels that would be congenial to a bishop, she asked the bishop what was his favorite text in the Bible. To her amazement he switched the question and insisted he preferred to learn what was her favorite text. It is doubtful whether she had one. There was a rather long pause, but then, rallying and brightening, she replied that the text in the Bible that had always specially appealed to her was, "They also serve who only stand and wait." "And what, my Lord," she repeated, "is your favorite text?" Whereupon, without even the suggestion of a smile, the bishop answered, "God tempers the wind to the shorn lamb." One grows less and less sure in telling that story that it will be appreciated as it ought to be. Even seminary students have been known to fail to grasp the point that neither quotation is from the Bible, the first being from John Milton and the second from Laurence Sterns (reported by Robert J. McCracken, *The Making of the Sermon*, p. 30).

Let the Word capture your heart and mind. Let your life be an unchained epistle of God. Let your witness of God's truth be your love of the scriptures.

Luther's love of Christ.

Luther addressed his faith. He discovered not wrath but love in Christ. St. Ambrose, in the fourth century, spoke these words: "I have nothing whereof I may glory in my works; I will therefore glory in Christ. I will not glory because I am righteous, but because I am redeemed; not because I am clear of sin, but because my sins are forgiven."

Luther found his peace in studying Romans. These words came from his life: "Where forgiveness of sins is, there is life and blessedness." Luther placed salvation entirely on grace, the undeserved love of God. Luther believed with Paul a person is justified by faith wrought by the divine spirit and word of grace, and that the Spirit of God then works inward righteousness in those who believe. Christ alone fulfilled the law and bore our sins. A person is justified, made right in the sight of God, by faith.

Luther derived love and strength from faith and delighted to do good. Christ, who dwells in a person through faith, accomplishes all and conquers all. The justified person's deeds are not for his own righteousness but for the service of God and others. All this grace is bestowed by the Word that dwells in Christ, the bread of life; and this bread of life is given outwardly in preaching and the Lord's Supper, and inwardly by "God's own teaching."

Luther sees the severity of sin — an unwillingness to meet God at the place where God has approached us. Sin is ingratitude, disobedience, and self-assertion. God has come in Jesus Christ to meet humankind. Christ is God.

Faith in Christ became the key to Luther's theology. "Stephen found in the Old Testament conclusive proof that Jesus was the Christ; but, many another Rabbi, and even Saint Paul himself before his vision at Damascus, found in the same Old Testament conclusive proof that Jesus was not the Christ. The miracles of Jesus and the authority of His teaching were proof to Nicodemus that Jesus was come from God; but to the other Pharisees they were proof that Jesus was come from the devil. To the reasonable Greek, Jesus was folly; to the religious Jew, Jesus was a scandal; and the 3,000 years of preparation seem to have been no help at all. He was revealed to faith alone" (D.T. Niles, *That They May Have Life*, p. 27).

The Reformation began with these affirmations: "Wretched man that I am! Who will rescue me from this body of death? Thanks be to God through Jesus Christ our Lord!" (Romans 7:24). "No, in all these things we are more than conquerors through him who loved us. For I am convinced that neither death, nor life, nor angels, nor rulers, nor things present, nor things to come, nor powers, nor height, nor depth, nor anything else in all creation, will be able to separate us from the love of God in Christ Jesus our Lord" (Romans 8:37-39). Faith is to accept God's offer of salvation and to live by it.

While the Reformation continued and Luther saw it was necessary to allow the new church to be born, he protested against the chosen name, "Lutheran." Luther's choice was to call it the "Christian church." Too bad they didn't accept his choice. Lutherans are not followers of Luther but followers of Christ.

The Reformation began and a new church was born. It was similar to a mountain climber in the Alps who had to sleep in a little chalet near the top of a mountain, heard before dawn a rolling, rumbling, roaring sound, asked: "Is it the end of the world?" The guide replied: "It is the sun melting the glacier on the other side of the mountain. It is not the end of the world but the beginning of a new day."

Luther's love of people.

The principles of the Reformation had been formed.

There is the formal or objective principle: the absolute supremacy of the Word. The canonical scriptures are the only infallible source and rule of faith, with the privilege and practice of the right of private interpretation.

There is the material or subject principle: a person is justified by grace. A person is freed of guilt and declared righteous by trusting in God above all things.

There is the social or ecclesiastical principle: the universal priesthood of believers, the right and duty of the Christian to read the Bible and to participate in the government and all public affairs of the church.

Before His ministry began, Jesus went into the wilderness. Before Paul preached Christ, he spent years of preparation in the wilderness. Luther began the constructive period of his career as a reformer while confined in the Wartburg Castle.

While in the Wartburg Castle Luther wrote concerning the priesthood of all believers. He contended that works were the spontaneous love in obedience to God. Someone has said, "A good or a bad house does not make a good or a bad builder, but a good or a bad builder makes a bad or a good house. In general, the work never makes the workman like itself, but the workman makes the work like himself."

What kind of work do you do? Lutherans often forget that works stem from faith. We cannot serve God while idle. "Thus you will know them by their fruits" (Matthew 7:20). We are to do good works. We are not to trust in good works to save us. The person who is saved does good works.

Where are your good works? In evangelism? "A man talks about the weather because he has nothing else to talk about. He talks about Jesus Christ because nothing else is worth talking

103

about. That kind of compulsion comes only to those who have felt the power of Christ at firsthand. Like men released from prison after all hope is gone, they cannot refrain from telling others about it, especially others who themselves are imprisoned" (Jesse M. Bader, *Evangelism in a Changing America*, p. 139).

Some worry about doing good works. The Bank of England was forced to employ a great many women instead of men who had gone into service with the armed forces during World War I. A young woman was assigned the task of detecting counterfeit notes. The Bank of England note was exceedingly difficult to counterfeit. This young lady had to examine piles of large bills. The task was affecting her nerves and she was near a nervous collapse. The superior officer of the bank saw her on the verge of tears and sought to comfort her. "Don't worry," he said, "when you come to a 'phoney' you will know it by the touch. It is this crinkliness of the paper that is so difficult to counterfeit. The touch instinctively discerns the difference when a counterfeit appears."

You can tell a Christian by Jesus Christ's touch. You will instinctively recognize a person of faith. Luther was such in his love of scripture, love of Christ, and love of people. Go and do likewise!

Sermon 17

Honoring the Saints

Text: Revelation 7:2-17

> "After this I looked, and there was a great multitude that no one could count, from every nation, from all tribes and peoples and languages, standing before the throne and before the Lamb, robed in white, with palm branches in their hands. They cried out in a loud voice, saying 'Salvation belongs to our God who is seated on the throne, and to the Lamb.'"
>
> — Revelation 7:9-10

The preacher is required to answer two questions on All Saints' Day: 1) What is the meaning of All Saints' Day? and 2) What is the book of Revelation about? The preacher's skill in answering these questions will be determined by the clarity of thought in the minds of worshipers when they leave the church. The preacher must not spend all the sermon time answering these introductory questions. The preacher must soon get to the main theme, "Honoring the Saints."

All Saints' Day is the day in the church year when we remember all the faithful departed and laud the triumph of Christ over all false gods. This festival of All Saints' has been celebrated in the church from the ninth century. It had its beginnings in 360 AD in Syria. The Greeks celebrated All Saints' Day during Chrysostom's life time (347?-407). It was a tribute to all martyrs who died believing in Jesus Christ.

In the Apostles' Creed we say we believe in "the communion of saints." "Saints" in the Protestant vocabulary is not always understood. "Saint" is a believer. In the creed we are confessing the truth expressed in the Apology of the Augsburg Confession: "We say and know certainly that this Church wherein saints live,

105

is and abides truly on earth, namely that some of God's children are here and there, in all the world, in various kingdoms, islands, lands and cities, from the rising of the sun to its setting, who have truly learned to know Christ and His Gospel."

The "invisible" church, known only by God, consists of past and present believers. We thank God for those who have remained faithful to God until death, by the power of Christ and His gospel.

We proceed to answer the complicated question regarding the book of Revelation. This last book of the Bible is misunderstood and read less than any other book in the Bible. It is either left untouched or believed to be some prediction of the future because of its language and complexity of thought.

It was written about 94 AD, supposedly by John the Apostle. Its symbolic language gives encouragement to Christians in a time of persecution. The writer to avoid Roman punishment wrote in language understood only by Christians. To make the book a long-distance lens whereby future events could be predicted is to make Revelation a fortune teller's book instead of focusing on the revelation of God to His people in a time of persecution.

We celebrate this day contemplating Revelation 7:2-17, which is the epistle for this occasion.

What was the multitude celebrating?

"... Standing before the throne and before the Lamb, robed in white, with palm branches in their hands."

Greeks and Romans used palms in celebrating military victories. Romans would shout in a chorus: "More than conquerors at last." Jewish reapers used palms rejoicing at the end of a harvest.

The multitude are the reapers in this chapter of Revelation. They have been true to Christ until death. They remained faithful although persecuted, taunted with the temptation to deny Christ and save themselves.

It was a message for those about to die. What are you sowing? Will it be a glad day for you to reap what you have sown?

It is a message for the living: What are you sowing?

Two men were discussing religion. One contended that a child should be given the privilege of deciding for himself or herself what religion to follow. They walked out of the house into the garden area. The one who contended a do-it-yourself religion was sufficient, noticed that his friend had many weeds in his garden and would have to dig them out. "But why?" said his friend: "Should not the garden decide for itself what should grow?" "But," his companion complained, "The garden will be nothing but weeds." "You have spoken rightly," said the friend, "and so it is with a child's life. Nothing remains but agnosticism unless the weeds of false religions are destroyed."

The question is: What are we sowing? The multitude bearing palms was celebrating the harvest, commemorating all that God had done for them:

> God had taken them through the wilderness;
> God had taken them from darkness and dreariness;
> God had preserved them through drought; and
> God had protected them from foes and fears.

From experiences of life, the multitude found reason to rejoice; they saw reason for thankfulness. "Salvation belongs to our God who is seated on the throne, and to the Lamb!" As John the Baptist had proclaimed: "Here is the Lamb of God who takes away the sin of the world!" (John 2:29) so this multitude could exclaim in unison, "Salvation belongs to our God...."

What do you see when you kneel at the altar? The cross of Jesus Christ, the sign of God's rule over all. What goes down your throat? Bread and wine, the body and blood of Jesus, the assurance of God's victory over sin and death. Thank God for His forgiveness and His real presence, "... for his steadfast love endures forever" (1 Chronicles 16:34).

The multitude stood before God.

The multitude stood before the throne because they were faithful over a few things. Their treasure was in their hearts, "For where your treasure is, there your heart will be also" (Matthew 6:21). They believed to have Christ in the heart gives strength. They stood before the throne in blessedness.

Note these words: "For this reason they are before the throne of God, and worship him day and night within his temple, and the one who is seated on the throne will shelter them" (7:15).

Whatever your thoughts of heaven, Revelation dispels any thought of idleness. It is an honor to serve God "day and night within his temple...."

We exist now in this age and on this earth, simply as an exercising ground. We are to cultivate our capacities on earth as an apprenticeship for heaven!

What kind of work are you doing? Is it the kind of work you will do when you pass beyond life's trivialities?

When we work day and night in the service for Christ and His church we know the presence of God. "... The one who is seated on the throne will shelter them." To be sheltered with His presence is to serve Him in faith. To be sheltered with Christ's presence is to know the meaning of His church's work. If you doubt the validity of your life, take up some service for God that is too big for you. Christ will bless you with His presence.

Life consists of too many trivialities. There is a danger in thinking what we do in the church is trifling. Put your hand on the plow and concentrate on those things that have meaning for your life and for the lives of others.

They were clothed with white robes.

The robe is the garment that is the result of deeds. These saints were robed in the purity of God because of their faithfulness. "White" is the symbol of purity, the kind of brilliance that overshadowed Jesus on the Mount of Transfiguration. It is like the brilliance reflected by the sun on snow.

Their robes were washed in the blood of the Lamb. The cleansing was not the result of their own effort. It was God's forgiveness that made them pure, white, lustrous.

God provides the means for cleansing; we employ them. "... They have washed their robes and made them white in the blood of the Lamb." They not only trusted Him for pardon; they trusted Him for purifying them.

Do you trust God that much? He has provided us cleansing in the word and the sacraments. Are you using them?

Every saint in that multitude bore a seal on his forehead, God's mark, like the mark we receive at baptism. Out of tribulation they came and washed their robes. They served God day and night. "For the Lamb at the center of the throne will be their shepherd, and he will guide them to springs of the water of life, and God will wipe every tear from their eyes" (7:17).

We can endure only in faith the worst days of testing. We can see only in faith the shepherd who leads us through the stormy and still waters. By the power of God, "Surely goodness and mercy shall follow... and we... shall dwell in the house of the Lord forever" (Psalm 23:6).

Sermon 18

To Whom Much Is Given

Text: Luke 12:42-48

"From everyone to whom much has been given, much will be required; and from the one to whom much has been entrusted, even more will be demanded."

— Luke 12:48

Jesus had just told the disciples the parable of the faithful and unfaithful servants. A tyrannical and drunken servant took advantage of his temporary authority while the master of a household was away. The unfaithful servant did not act according to the will of the master. And Jesus said, "From everyone to whom much has been given, much will be required." It is a warning to be ready for the coming of the Lord. It could be directly addressed to the religious leaders of Jesus' day. Peter said, "Lord, are you telling us this parable for us or for everyone?" Jesus said, "Who then is the faithful and prudent manager whom his master will put in charge of his slaves, to give them their allowance of food at the proper time? Blessed is that slave whom his master will find at work when he arrives. Truly, I tell you, he will put that one in charge of all his possessions" (Luke 12:41-44).

Christians need to answer these questions: What will we be doing when Christ comes again? What has been given to us that requires response to God?

We have been given time.

An Asian writer lays this charge at our doors: "You call your thousand material devices 'labor-saving machinery,' yet you are forever busy. With the multiplying of your machinery you grow increasingly fatigued, anxious, nervous, dissatisfied. Whatever you have, you want more; and wherever you are, you want to go somewhere else. You have a machine to dig the raw material for you... a machine to manufacture it... a machine to transport it... a machine to sweep and dust, one to carry messages, one to write, one to talk, one to sing, one to play at the theater, one to vote, one to sew... and a hundred others to do a hundred other things for you, and still you are the most nervously busy man in the world... Your devices are neither time-saving nor soul-saving machinery. They are so many sharp spurs which urge you on to invent more machinery and to do more business" (cited by George Buttrick, *Parables of Jesus*, p. 134).

The charge is difficult to refute. No one would advocate turning back the clock. Many lives support the contention that with time-saving devices they have less time for God. Another Oriental accompanying a New Yorker on a subway ride changing from one subway to another and to another to save three minutes, exclaimed at the end of the ride: "What are you going to do with those three minutes?"!

What are you doing with the time God has allotted you on earth? How many fathers and mothers spend all their time making a living, making it more comfortable for the family and for themselves, while the children grow up without guidance and without God?

The way we spend our time says something about us. The main business of living is not to be a lawyer or architect or computer expert or a plumber or a salesperson — but to love God with your whole heart and mind and spirit, and to love your neighbor.

Wrote Truman B. Douglas, "One of the most terrifying commentaries on the life of our time is a brief description, in the novel *The Man in the Gray Flannel Suit*, a description of a street in an American suburb. It was a street where nobody wished or intended to stay with the purpose of having a home. The families occupying the houses were only waiting, waiting to be able to afford a house in a neighborhood with more prestige. The big parties were the moving-out parties. 'On Greentree Avenue,' wrote Sloan Wilson, 'contentment was an object of contempt.' To be so obsessed with the need of being somewhere else, of getting ahead not to satisfy one's real needs and longings but to satisfy the conventional standards of our time, so that there can be no inward serenity, no enjoyment of friends and family and human warmth in themselves, so that contentment is contemptible, that is really terrifying" (*Why Go to Church?*, p. 116).

Do church people think differently? Church people could redeem the times. How many ministers and lay leaders of congregations have to plead and beg members of the church to do work for God? "I don't have time" is the answer they receive from well-meaning church people.

"To whom much is given!" In the fullness of time God sent His Son and it is our responsibility to tell others about His victory over evil and death. God will hold us accountable for our time on this earth. What are you doing with the time God has given you?

We have been given ability.

There are diversities of gifts but we all have the same Lord, claimed Saint Paul in 1 Corinthians 12:4. Whatever gift or talent God has given you, whether it be one or ten, is to be used for God. Blessings have been given to us by God. We are all tempted to think of them mostly as given for our enjoyment. A Christian receives nothing for himself or herself alone. God entrusts each person with a portion of talent.

Alexader Maclaren in his *Expositions of Holy Scripture* declares "Ungirt loins, unlit lamps, unused talents, sink a man like lead. Doing nothing is enough for ruin."

Why did the man in Jesus' parable of the talents (Matthew 25:14-30) bury it? He was afraid. "So I was afraid, and I went and hid your talent in the ground." Fear paralyzes service, cuts the nerve of activity, makes a person shun obedience. What he did wasn't logical. He was saying that his master's requirements were so great that he could not attempt to fulfill them. He should have said that because the requirements were so great, he would bend every effort to do his master's will.

But he was afraid! Some good church people are afraid. They say, "I can't go out and make visits. There are others more capable than I." Scripture states, "Perfect love casts out fear..." (1 John 4:18). Love is fruitful. Love moves a believer to action. The main reason why great numbers of church people do so little for God is because their hearts have never been touched with the thorough conviction that God has done everything, and invites us to love Him back.

Christians, lift up the cross and let it silence your doubts. Love God back. "We love because he first loved us" (1 John 4:19). Such love will be productive. Such love keeps commandments. Such love uses God-given talent.

Someone has said, "You can't put a live chick under a dead hen." As for the knowledge of God and how to lead others to Christ and His church, many a congregation is a dead hen (paraphrase of Shoemaker, *By the Power of God*, p. 106).

Some never work at Christianity. They breathe, eat, sleep, go to the office, fall in love, get married, have children, and die. Woe to us if that is all we do. God help us if we forsake God.

We have been given possessions.

There is a story of a cannibal who laid claim to a plot of land on the score of having swallowed the original owner! (Buttrick, *Who Owns the Earth?*, p. 92).

Could that be a commentary on our life. God is the owner. We are the tenants. The tenant often acts like the owner. Listen to the words of the owner: "But strive first for the kingdom of God and his righteousness, and all these things will be given to you as well" (Matthew 6:33). Again, "Do not store up for yourselves treasures on earth, where moth and rust consume and where thieves break in and steal; but store up for yourselves treasures in heaven, where neither moth nor rust consumes and where thieves do not break in and steal. For where your treasure is, there your heart will be also" (Matthew 6:19-21). Again, "No one can serve two masters; for a slave will either hate the one and love the other, or be devoted to one and despise the other. You cannot serve God and wealth" (Matthew 6:24).

Our greatest need is not bread but God. Bread was not Jesus' greatest need during His temptation. Jesus craved the Father's companionship. Bread satisfies momentarily.

Our greatest need is not a new automobile or a new dress or a new toy. Our greatest need is God.

113

Many Christians compromise life and have watered down the word of God. Tithing is often considered old-fashioned. People say, "It does not apply to modern times."

Has God changed? No. People change. The ideals of Christianity are of enduring quality. There is an epidemic of neutral living. Remember what Jesus said, "Whoever is not with me is against me, and whoever does not gather with me scatters" (Matthew 12:30). Jesus calls us to see that our greatest need is answered in Him. It is a matter of trust.

Everything belongs to God. We can't steal anything from Him. We can't put talents in our pockets. We are God's children. It is not too much to expect Christians to give a good portion of their time to Christ and His church. It is not too much to expect Christians to give their talents and service to Christ and His church. It is not too much to expect Christians to give a sizeable portion of their income for the preservation and extension of the kingdom.

Much is expected of Christians. Christians have been given the word and the sacraments. We have been given time, ability, and possessions. Much is required since so much has been given to us. God cannot expect too much of His believers.

Sermon 19

Confession for Young and Older

Text: Matthew 10:32-33

"Everyone therefore who acknowledges me before others, I also will acknowledge before my Father in heaven; but whoever denies me before others, I also will deny before my Father in heaven."

— Matthew 10:32-33

Walter Scott Athearn, one of America's foremost leaders in Christian education of a generation ago, once said, "If a boy or girl is not won for Christ by the time he or she is 21, the chances are three to one that he or she will not be won by anyone, anytime, anywhere." That statement frightens me.

Confessing belief in Jesus Christ was dangerous in the days of the early church. Yet, Christians confessed belief in Christ and many met their death by the jaws of a lion. It was dangerous to confess Christ in Europe during the Nazi era. It was difficult to confess Christ in communist Russia. Is it difficult to confess Christ in America?

The duty and delight in confessing Christ.

Do we readily confess faith in Jesus? Or do we rather air our doubts? Some say, "I am not a very good Christian, but..." If the sentence were completed it might continue, "I would not overcharge my customers... I would never be an oily church hypocrite like somebody I know." Such a person may not acknowledge Christ but will exalt some Christian virtues they possess or criticize someone else for not being as Christian.

It is not possible to be half pagan and half Christian. We cannot hold contradictory views of life. Truth cannot contradict

115

itself. The Christian is required to burn his bridges behind him. For better or worse I believe that Christ "is what God means by 'Man.' He is what man means by God" (J.S. Whale, *Christian Doctrine*, p. 104).

It is difficult to confess Christ in America. We confess less than what we believe. A young man said, "I do not pretend to be a Christian." No one should pretend to be more than what he or she believes. And no one should pretend to be less than what he or she believes.

It is our duty and delight to confess Christ. We cannot separate daily living from God. There is danger in half profession, or in a formalism that chokes faith. Public profession of Christ is the very substance of judgment. There is "... joy in heaven over one sinner who repents...." (Luke 15:7). There must be joy in heaven over one who confesses the creed, "I believe in Jesus Christ...." Surely Christ responds, "I believe in that person." The event is seen in another world when we confess Christ by word and deed!

Some will ask, "Are not deeds better than words?" Homer's heroes move in strong silence while his cowards chatter like blue jays. The "strong, silent man" bit can be overdone. A hero need not act like a deaf mute. Sometimes the hand's deed cannot become known without the lip's deed.

It would have to be publicized if a cure for cancer were found. Sometimes we can do nothing but speak. When Peter and John went up to the Temple to pray, a man lame from birth asked them for alms. Peter said, "I have no silver or gold, but what I have I give you; in the name of Jesus Christ of Nazareth, stand up and walk" (Acts 3:6). The lame man walked!

Confessing Christ should gather all our deeds, but it should also bring words of confidence, hope, and courage. "Whoever denies me before others..." Jesus said. We are apt to cringe when we hear that statement. However, if a person becomes a stranger to the upper dimensions of truth and love, he is estranged from himself, from his neighbor, and from God whom he has denied.

What the confession may mean.
Abraham Holmes, the Puritan, refused to confess any king but Jesus. He was tried for treachery in London and sentenced

to be hung. The horses became fractious when they took him in a wagon to the gallows. So Holmes said: "Stop, gentlemen, let me go afoot. Remember how the ass saw God, whom the prophet could not see. There is more in this than you think."

There is more in this confession than we may think. Jesus said it may "... set a man against his father, and a daughter against her mother, and a daughter-in-law against her mother-in-law; and one's foes will be members of one's own household" (Matthew 10:35-36). Believing in Jesus Christ may disrupt your household. Believing in Jesus Christ may alter your choice of friends. Believing in Jesus Christ means rearranging your business and social life. "Those who find their life will lose it, and those who lose their life for my sake will find it" (Matthew 10:39).

Constantine after he became Emperor sent priests to a tribe of Goths on the north shore of the Black Sea. The chief of the tribe had sent a deputation to him explaining that a Christian slave girl, whom they had captured in a raid, had converted them. A slave girl — there could be no better symbol of human helplessness — because she was a Christian belonged to the operation of the gospel. There that same power that raised Jesus from the dead was at work, and by her witness that power leaped out in dynamic activity (paraphrase of D.T. Niles, *That They May Live*, p. 53).

Confessing Christ means you have found your life. In slavery, in an office building or in the field, the power of confessing Christ can change a tribe or the world.

Youth is a time of confession. Every age has confession time. Our task is to keep young in the faith. Our lives are to have freshness of conviction, sincerity, and courage.

We admire youth's energy. Our bodies wear out. Faith never wears out. We need perspectives of God-given faith.

Did you read Professor Gordon Blackwell's story of the tuba player who had played his instrument in one band for twenty years? "Finally, one day he had a chance to go to the back of the auditorium and hear the band for the first time from a distance. Excitedly, the tuba player rushed up to the bandmaster and exclaimed: 'Man, that was great! All my life I've thought that The Stars and Stripes Forever went um-pah, um-pah, um-pah. You

117

know, it really goes, and he hummed the tune, Da da, da da did da, da did da' " (Maclennan, *Pastoral Preaching*, p. 50).

The voices of Christian people confessing Christ as Lord of all can put heavenly music into our national life. The individual hearing only his own voice drowns out others. God hears all the voices together. In the frame of eternity God says, "... I will acknowledge before my Father in heaven...."

Sermon 20

Jeremiah and the New Covenant

Text: Jeremiah 31:31-34

The days are surely coming, says the Lord, when I will make a new covenant with the house of Israel and the house of Judah. It will not be like the covenant that I made with their ancestors when I took them by the hand to bring them out of the land of Egypt — a covenant that they broke, though I was their husband, says the Lord. But this is the covenant that I will make with the house of Israel after those days, says the Lord: I will put my law within them, and I will write it on their hearts; and I will be their God, and they shall be my people. No longer shall they teach one another, or say to each other, "Know the Lord," for they shall know me, from the least of them to the greatest, says the Lord; for I will forgive their iniquity, and remember their sin no more.

The old and new testaments are connected with a covenant. A covenant is an agreement or compact between individuals. In scripture the covenant is between God and His people. There were covenants between Abraham and the Amorites (Genesis 14:13); a covenant between Abraham and Abimelech (Genesis 21:27); a covenant between Laban and Jacob (Genesis 31:44); a covenant between Jonathan and David (1 Samuel 18:3); and, a covenant between Solomon and Hiram (1 Kings 5:2-6).

Covenants were sealed by swallowing a drop of each other's blood in primitive times. Later, it was refined to exchanging handclasps. People shaking hands today are not only greeting one another but signifying friendship, a covenant to remain friends.

Jeremiah lived during the subjection of Jerusalem in 609 BC, its capture in 598 BC, and its destruction in 587 BC. Jeremiah is often referred to as the "weeping prophet." Jeremiah's message

119

was sober like an Amos or Isaiah. Jeremiah announced that the day of God would not be a day of victory and rejoicing but a dark, bitter day of gloom.

Jeremiah referred to the covenant made at Sinai where the people promised to worship only Yahweh and Yahweh (God) covenanted to bring His people into Canaan, according to Exodus 34. Jeremiah preached a new covenant of spiritual awareness and the need for salvation. Although Israel had broken her covenant with God, God was willing to write into their hearts a new pact that would be available to every person.

The New Testament covenant, which Jesus spoke of in Matthew 26:27-28, is what Jeremiah prepared us for: "Drink from it, all of you; for this is my blood of the covenant, which is poured out for many for the forgiveness of sins."

What is written on your heart?

The ten commandments were written in stone at Sinai. Jeremiah claimed that was not enough. The commandments must be written upon your heart in order to be effective. Jeremiah knew how wicked and weak their hearts were. "The sin of Judah is written with an iron pen; with a diamond point it is engraved on the tablet of their hearts..." (Jeremiah 17:1).

We are surprised at the foolishness of the people of ancient Troy. They withstood the assault of the Greeks for a long time, but one day they allowed a large, wooden horse to enter their city, containing enemy soldiers. At night, the soldiers emerged from the horse, and threw open the gates of the city. The canny Greeks poured in and were victorious.

Jeremiah knew the "wooden horse" had entered the life of Israel. Jesus knew the "wooden horse" had entered the religious life of the Jews. The "wooden horse" for us can be the ten commandments written in a book but not written in our hearts.

The new covenant Jesus wrote in his own blood. His words from the mountain ring out: "Therefore, whoever breaks one of the least of these commandments, and teaches others to do the same, will be called least in the kingdom of heaven, but whoever does them and teaches them will be called great in the kingdom of heaven. For I tell you, unless your righteousness exceeds that of the scribes and Pharisees, you will never enter the kingdom of heaven" (Matthew 5:19-20).

Does our righteousness exceed that of the good people in this world who worship their own goodness and not God? Does our righteousness tower over the evil of this world? Jesus said to " '... love the Lord your God with all your heart, and with all your soul, and with all your mind.' This is the greatest and first commandment. And a second is like it: 'You shall love your neighbor as yourself.' On these two commandments hang all the law and the prophets" (Matthew 22:37-40).

God has written this new covenant in blood. When the commandments are written in our hearts, by the blood of the Lamb, righteousness can be true.

Paschal, French philosopher (1623-1662, *Thoughts*, p. 521), said, "The law demands what it cannot give. Grace gives what it demands." The New Testament Christian has the law written in his heart by the love of God. Paul wrote of it in 2 Corinthians 3:3, "You yourselves are our letter, written on our hearts, to be known and read by all; and you show that you are a letter of Christ, prepared by us, written not with ink but with the Spirit of the living God, not on tablets of stone but on tablets of human hearts."

Forgiveness is poured into your heart.

The misery of people without God is characterized by self-love, contradictions, and inconsistency in their lives. They grow weary in doing good. They are forever restless, like the tiger prancing to and fro in his cage.

Oh, the happiness of people with God! We cannot keep the commandments simply by mere affirmation and determination. But in our despair we do not become despondent. We are not forsaken in our failure. We are not abandoned in our sin. God has made a new covenant. Every time Christians partake of the Sacrament of the Lord's Supper, they partake of the new covenant, "shed for the remission of sins."

When the Christian takes the bread and lifts the cup to his lips, he can hear Jeremiah's words of Yahweh: "... I will be their God, and they shall be my people... for I will forgive their iniquity, and I will remember their sin no more."

The Advent season is preparation for the second coming of Christ. Advent prepares us for the rightful celebration of Christ's birthday. His people remember the covenant, purchased with His own blood.

Write this truth upon your heart. God pours forgiveness into your heart. As the liturgy declares, "The body and blood of our Lord Jesus Christ strengthen and keep you in His grace."

Sermon 21

With One Voice

Text: Romans 15:4-13

"May the God of steadfastness and encouragement grant you to live in harmony with one another, in accordance with Christ Jesus, so that together you may with one voice glorify God and Father of our Lord Jesus Christ."

— Romans 15:5-6

Paul wrote a letter to a church in Rome he had never visited and had not established. This epistle ranks first among Paul's writings in the New Testament. It was written at Corinth sometime between 54 and 58 AD. Paul had already been a missionary twenty years. He had only six to ten years of life left.

He had finished his work in Asia Minor and Greece and wanted to travel farther west. It was only natural for him to stop at Rome and visit the church there, since he planned to go to Spain.

Paul had been laboring under great pressure for several years, his other letters, Galatians and Corinthians, indicated. Paul considered himself primarily an itinerant missionary. He did not like to build on other men's foundations or his own. The care of the churches was oppressive. Galatians and Corinthians refer to his travels, his anxieties, and his activities. His major work was occupied with the disastrous rift between the conservative body of Christians who held their allegiance to Jerusalem and the new Gentile Christians. Paul's work had been misunderstood and opposed by many Jewish Christians. Paul began raising an offering from among the Gentile churches for the relief of the poverty-stricken Christians in Jerusalem.

A person should read the writings of Paul if doubting the importance of benevolence and support of overseas missionaries.

123

Romans, the longest and most theological book of all Paul's writings, is essential for the Christian mind. He closes his exhortation to the factions in the Roman Church with a plea for unity. "May the God of steadfastness and encouragement grant you to live in harmony with one another, in accordance with Christ Jesus, so that together you may with one voice glorify the God and Father of our Lord Jesus Christ." Paul's words could be translated, "May the God from whom come the endurance and the comfort grant unto you minds at harmony with one another and with Christ Jesus." If this occurs, they will be united and with "one voice" speak to the community of God's glory.

With one voice, speak of the strength and encouragement which comes from the scriptures.

"For whatever was written in former days was written for our instruction, so that by steadfastness and by the encouragement of the scriptures we might have hope."

The American Bible Society always asks churches to observe a Sunday emphasizing the importance of the scriptures. These words in Romans compel us to dwell upon the importance of the scriptures.

The scriptures encourage us by recording events in the lives of people who have been beset by the mystery of pain and sorrow, and by cruel partings from loved ones. We remember poor Abraham, with calm sorrow, laying wife Sarah in the cave at Macpelah. We remember Jacob, with his weak eyes in agony when Rachel died. The struggle of grief and faith in Mary and Martha's hearts when their brother died. The psalms speak of life's deepest experiences. For the afflicted in mind and body, Psalms contain a special message. The strength of Job has strengthened many a sufferer to endure.

We children of the faith need these living examples of scripture to tell us repeatedly how God has sustained people.

Not only does scripture tell us of all the complications of human affairs, which we experience, but shows us the source of strength. It challenges humanity and bares the innermost motive power. It shows us sorrow and the power of faith, and the source and purpose of God. No person need fear or faint before torture and disaster. Our healing comes from something more universal than philosophy; it comes from God. God comes with patience and steadfastness.

It is tantalizing to endure and patiently submit to murmurings. That is only half the lesson. The solemn pressure of what we ought to do is heavy on the sorrowful and on the happy heart. Our responsibilities to others do not cease because our hearts may be heavy or our lives darkened. Many have their strength sapped by mere endurance. You do well if you do not falter under your burden, but you do better if you plod steadily along. Things are heaviest when you stand still. Do not cease to toil because you suffer. You will feel pain more if you do. Take the encouragement from the scriptures. Allow the scriptures to lead and make you steadfast, "For whatever was written... for our instruction...."

The scriptures exhort, summon us to silence, command us to conscience by Jesus' pattern of pure motives, which He gives. We are called to be followers of Christ, not of Apollos or Cephas or Paul or Luther, but of Christ. Accept the promises of encouragement and steadfastness by faith. With one voice proclaim God of the scriptures!

With one voice speak of the hope that fills you with joy and peace in believing.

Encouragement and steadfastness, produced by scripture, lead us to hope. If by the power of God, I am able by God's power not only to endure but to toil, I have evidence that God's power will help me look forward through any storm.

Alexander Maclaren, famous for his *Expositions of Scripture*, wrote "The lion once slain houses a swarm of bees who lay up honey in its carcass. The trial borne with brave persistence yields a story of sweet hopes. If we can look back and say, 'Thou hast been with me in six troubles,' it is good logic to look forward and say, 'and in seven Thou wilt not forsake me.' "

Notice how the Apostle Paul defines for us the conditions of hope — the "joy and peace in believing, so that by the power of the Holy Spirit you may abound in hope" (Romans 15:13).

It is in believing, not in certain exercises of the mind, that these blessings are realized. Many resort to daydreaming or use

125

tranquilizers. Their favorite subject of contemplation is the evils in their hearts. We are tempted to grasp any thought for peace of mind. You will not know the joy and peace in believing if you are thinking more of your own imperfections instead of the pardon of Christ. You will not enjoy the fruit of faith if you dwell more on the imperfections of your own love of Christ rather than the perfectness of His love. You cannot know the joy of believing if you are only absorbed in self-examination and do not practice your faith. Blessings come by believing. Belief results in joy and peace when you trust God.

Remember, the Christian carries with him or her the pledge of eternity. God has pledged a resurrection like Christ's resurrection. The sorrows of this earthly experience and the joys of the Christian life blend together to produce one blessed result of hope that is full of certainty for living this life, and the assurance of another life with God forever!

The God of hope reminds us of the vast difference the gospel makes in our outlook on life. The gospel delivers us from the gloom enfolding our minds when we trust human factors. We see what God has done for human beings in Christ. He redeems the individual's life. He transforms the nature of the church. He uncovers limitless possibilities that our minds can explore but never exhaust. All the resources of God are offered to the believer in Christ. God offers us the joy and peace in believing while the world offers nothing but threats. The working of the Holy Spirit saves us from life's formal blankness and blackness. God's hope enlarges our hope. Only God's presence in us can give us the gifts of new life and hope.

With One Voice, let the church speak of the God of hope, who beckons us to remember there is a second coming of Christ.

Sermon 22

Prepare the Way

Text: Isaiah 40:1-8

"Comfort, O comfort my people, says your God. Speak tenderly to Jerusalem, and cry to her that she has served her term, that her penalty is paid, that she has received from the Lord's hand double for all her sins. A voice cries out: 'In the wilderness prepare the way of the Lord, make straight in the desert a highway for our God. Every valley shall be lifted up, and every mountain and hill be made low, the uneven ground shall become level, and the rough places a plain. Then the glory of the Lord shall be revealed, and all people shall see it together, for the mouth of the Lord has spoken.' A voice says, 'Cry out!' And I said, 'What shall I cry?' All people are grass, their constancy is like the flower of the field. The grass withers, the flower fades, when the breath of the Lord blows upon it; surely the people are grass. The grass withers, the flower fades; but the word of our God will stand forever.' "

People's names have meaning. The Hebrews attached significance to people's names. One of the greatest prophets among the Hebrews, Isaiah, means "Jehovah is salvation." He so strongly influenced prophecy that the works of anonymous writers who followed him were associated with his name. The words of this text are the words from "Second Isaiah": "In the wilderness prepare the way of the Lord..." (Isaiah 40:3).

Second Isaiah, an unknown writer, through his monotheism provided the basis for the theology of the cross. His interpretation of suffering, its purifying and redeeming effects on Israel and on the world, made Christ's death on the cross an acceptable truth. Christianity cannot be fully understood without Second Isaiah. Isaiah is the most evangelical of all the prophets.

127

With the fall of Jerusalem in 586 BC and the deportation of the best of its population to Babylon, some Jews questioned the validity of their national God. With the fall of Jerusalem this increased the appeal of the Babylonian religion. Second Isaiah faced this danger. He proclaimed one God, the omnipotent, who would deliver His people. He preached a gospel of joy and sorrow, defeat and disaster. God's care of His people is tender. Their sin in worshiping like the Babylonians hurt His love.

God is preparing the way for His people.

Do you believe God is active in current events? What has God done? What is God doing? What is God about to do?

The Bible looks upon all events of humankind under the providential control of God. Our willfulness thwarts God's design and purpose. God comes on the scene.

God entered the life of a wayward man, Saul of Tarsus, and the work of Paul changed Asia Minor and Greece. God entered the life of murderer Moses, and led the people of Israel from Egypt. God influenced the life of Isaiah: "Then I heard the voice of the Lord saying, 'Whom shall I send, and who will go for us?' And I said, 'Here am I; send me!' " (Isaiah 6:8). As Cyrus is sweeping over empires in western Asia in the sixth century BC, and Babylon is about to fall, this prophet hears a voice: "In the wilderness prepare the way of the Lord"!

It seems impossible that they will be set free, according to Second Isaiah, restored to their homeland and again have national independence.

The voice does not ask them to make ready a highway. It is not even a highway for their own journey. Forces beyond their knowledge or control, the forces of history, ultimately God Himself, are preparing a way by which God will arrive and lead them.

Second Isaiah uses poetry. Valleys will be lifted up, mountains and hills will be lowered, rough terrain will be made a plain. There are no ranges of mountains between Babylon and Jerusalem! There are political, physical, psychological, theological difficulties that are filling Israelite minds with forebodings.

God will respond to His people's hearts. The military successes of Cyrus, the downfall of their captors, the diplomatic negotiations will result in liberty. This will have a spiritual impact. The living God is the mover of hearts who acts in history.

Do you believe God controls this old world of ours? Carlyle wrote to Froude his gloomy view of God, "He does nothing." Zola likened the movement of human affairs to a railway train: "The train is the world; we are the freight; fate is the track; death is the darkness; God is the engineer — who is dead."

Second Isaiah faced this kind of materialism. We do not have the ability or energy to overcome such obstacles. We need somebody who initiates. God prepares the highway in the wilderness of sin and human history. God will reveal His glory, "... the word of our God will stand forever" (Isaiah 40:8).

This prophet tells the people who God is. He is the omnipotent, omniscient, loving God. God enters the scene so that our efforts are never without results. God will restore His people. The return journey will be hard but God will lead.

When we speak of the God of love, we must also speak of God as *able*. Who would trust his life to an incompetent? People often acknowledge a power behind events but are they sure that power has a heart? The Christian says "yes." When we speak of the God of the heart, we also speak of the God of might.

Just before the Russians conquered the city of Breslau, on the last Sunday when the congregation was permitted to worship in the St. Elizabeth Church, their pastor told his people:

> "One and a half years ago, when the Russians arrived, the church had to stay in order to officiate as long as any of the people of the community remained here and were in need of the aid and comfort of the Gospel. And lo and behold! God richly blessed the hard work of the Evangelical Church in the period of siege and occupation... If, nevertheless, all human hopes which we cherished for our homeland are frustrated, if our community buildings and churches are taken from us, if one street after another is evacuated... God doesn't take without giving at the same time. He doesn't demand the grave of sacrifice of homelessness without ennobling us at the same time with a great task and endowing us with the promise of His blessing if we will but trust in Him...eternal goodness... Thus being called, we are going to bid farewell to our beloved

Silesia, if this is God's will; farewell as it must be also from our beloved Elizabeth Church, which like a mother, has nurtured our soul. We have to thank God for what he has entrusted to us. May He hold us in His arms and guide us."

This gospel Second Isaiah preached. That kind of gospel is preached from this pulpit — the gospel of the God of love who is able.

The cry of His people.
"A voice says, 'Cry out!' And I said, 'What shall I cry?' " (Isaiah 40:6).

Our generation is vexed by fears that also obsessed these captives of Babylon. Scientific advances have furnished the means by which civilization can be destroyed. We dread the machinations of aloof and secretive powers. We dread enslavement by an economic tyranny contemptuous of our morals and derisive of our venerated pieties. We dream economic collapse that might plunge our own country and the world into chaos.

How many of us are vexed by trivial fears? What will our neighbors think of us? Haunted by anxiety to be liked by certain people and afraid we will not? Whether we wear clothes that are still in fashion?

What is the Christian's cry? "All people are grass, their constancy is like the flower of the field. The grass withers, the flower fades; but the word of our God will stand forever" (Isaiah 40:7-8).

There are moments in us when we worship humankind's capacities and advances into the unknown. Human beings seem so efficient that religion seems irrelevant. Human beings often conclude they can manage their own affairs and shape their own destiny.

There are moments in us when we despise human beings and in turn despise the God who made them. When thousands and thousands of years roll on, how ridiculously small are these trifling fears of people. We have to say with the poet Tennyson, "However we brave it out, we men are a little breed."

This prophet wants us to recognize the finiteness of people and the infiniteness of God, the role of our creatureliness in the history of obedience to the word of a righteous God. "And the world and its desire are passing away, but those who do the will of God live forever" (1 John 2:17).

The Advent cry.

Christ could come again in the midst of preparations for Christmas. Then what would you think of the Christmas list still incomplete? Then what would you think of the Christmas cards yet to be sent? Then what would you think of the tree yet to be decorated? The list, the cards, the tree would seem inconsequential, wouldn't they?!

During the Advent season be not lost in your own preparations to celebrate. That event for which you plan to celebrate was prepared long ago so that in preparations for an annual anniversary you will not be lost in preparation but found believing in Christ.

Christ could come again in the world of cold suspicion and threats of war. Then what would you think of people in other lands? Then what would you think of a trip to the moon? Then what would you think of the weapons monopolizing our national budget? Countries, space trips, weapons would seem inconsequential.

God came to this earth in the form of a baby, in the fullness of time. Isn't it high time for followers of God to think and live in belief of this act of God in history? Isn't it time for believers to quit crying despair and bend the knee in adoration? Isn't it time to quit crying, "Where is God?" and to confess, "God be merciful to me a sinner"?

If you are going to be anxious about how things will ultimately result, have anxiety about your own soul and anxiety about any soul who disregards God. "... The word of our God will stand forever" (Isaiah 40:8). God has prepared a highway to the soul of every person. That highway began in eternity and is visible at Calvary. It took the point of the cross to plough that highway. God has already won the victory over evil and death. Let the cry of the redeemed be, "I know that my Redeemer lives."

"Comfort, O comfort my people, says your God" (Isaiah 40:1).

Sermon 23

What Christ Is Like
— A Shepherd

Text: Isaiah 40:9-11

> "Get you up to a high mountain, O Zion, herald of good tidings; lift up your voice with strength, O Jerusalem, herald of good tidings, lift it up, do not fear; say to the cities of Judah, 'Here is your God!'
>
> See, the Lord God comes with might, and his arm rules for him, and his recompense before him.
>
> He will feed his flock like a shepherd; he will gather the lambs in his arms, and carry them in his bosom, and gently lead the mother sheep."

In Tolstoy's moving book *War and Peace*, one of the most memorable scenes describes the night at Russian Headquarters when a messenger brought to Koutouzow, the old Commander-in-Chief, the first news of Napolean's retreat from Moscow. "After years of terrible strain and agony to which the soul of Russia had been subjected, the tidings sounded incredible. The envoy finished his report and waited for orders. There was nothing but silence. A staff officer was about to speak, but Koutouzow checked him with his hand. Koutouzow attempted to say something. Not a word would come. Finally, the old man turned away to where the sacred images stood against the wall. And, then, suddenly and unrestrainedly cried, 'Great God, my Lord and Creator! Thou hast heard my prayer! Russia is saved!' And, then, he burst into tears."

The prophet in Isaiah brings tidings more tender and wonderful: "Get you up to a high mountain, O Zion, herald of good tidings; lift up your voice with strength, O Jerusalem, herald of good tidings, lift it up, do not fear; say to the cities of Judah, 'Here is your God!' " (Isaiah 40:9).

The prophet could visualize distant Jerusalem which lay in ruins. The prophet knew that most of the exiles had never seen it. Jerusalem! Jerusalem! Jerusalem lived as a hallowed symbol of freedom-loving people. Its capture and devastation by enemies, followed by years of bitter strife by its people in Babylonian captivity, stood as the symbol of a sacred capital. More than a symbol, Jerusalem stood for a nation in covenant with God. The prophet hails her in a new role, destined to affect the whole world: "O Jerusalem, herald of good tidings, lift it up, do not fear; say to the cities of Judah, 'Here is your God!' "

Judah was enslaved. The prophet knew the people's conscience could not be aroused with an apologetic tone. His message was not what people should be and do. His message was one of boldness, in the sight of all people, asserting a gospel, affirming the presence of the redeeming Creator, "Here is your God!" This was the prophet's God.

What is your God like?

The God of many nominal Christians today is a god who is incapable of anger. He is a magnificent over-sized portrait of a sentimental human father who is incapable of the slightest desire to discipline His children. The reasoning of the average Christian father stems from the argument that his own sentimental affection for his children actually guarantees the happy eternal destiny of everybody. He assumes that love means the same thing for God and himself.

The "God" of many sin-enslaved people received impetus by the philosophy of Rabbi Liebmann. It would not be facetious to say with Walter Barlow in his book *God so Loved* that they would bid the modern prodigal to arise and go, not to his father, but to his psychiatrist, and say, "Doctor, I have developed a neurosis; it may even turn into a psychosis, and I am no more able to go peacefully about my chosen activities. Oh, rid me of my maladjustments. Restore to me my peace of mind, and make me as one of your successful patients" (p. 18).

What is your God like?

133

God is like a shepherd.

The prophet said, "... See, the Lord God comes with might, and his arm rules for him... He will feed his flock like a shepherd..." (Isaiah 40:10-11).

God is like a shepherd for the Christian. The shepherd of shepherds, the shepherd of sheep, was visible in a manger. That shepherd grew in physical stature, human and divine, to say: "I am the good shepherd. I know my own and my own know me, just as the Father knows me and I know the Father. And I lay down my life for the sheep" (John 10:14-15).

In Christ is the God we know. "Go and tell John what you hear and see: the blind receive their sight, the lame walk, the lepers are cleansed, the deaf hear, the dead are raised, and the poor have good news brought to them. And blessed is anyone who takes no offense at me" (Matthew 11:4-5).

There is your God. He is like a shepherd. He binds up the wounds of his sheep and tenderly carries the young.

John replied to the Pharisees, "I baptize with water. Among you stands one whom you do not know, the one who is coming after me; I am not worthy to untie the thong of his sandal" (John 1:26-27).

Do you know Christ, the great shepherd of the sheep?

When he came to Ephesus Paul found some disciples. He asked them, "Did you receive the Holy Spirit when you became believers? They replied, 'No, we have not even heard that there is a Holy Spirit.' Then he said, 'Into what then were you baptized?' They answered, 'Into John's baptism.' Paul said, 'John baptized with the baptism of repentance, telling the people to believe in the one who was to come after him that is, in Jesus.' On hearing this, they were baptized in the name of the Lord Jesus. When Paul had laid his hands on them, the Holy Spirit came upon them..." (Acts 19:2-6).

These disciples of Ephesus did not know Christ until they were baptized in the name of the great shepherd.

Have any of you been baptized in the name of anything or anyone other than Christ? Have any of you been brainwashed by the religious sciences of our day? Have you received the spirit of peace of mind and the Holy Spirit? Jesus said, "Beware of false prophets, who come to you in sheep's clothing but inwardly are ravening wolves" (Matthew 7:15). Could He not have said, "Beware of those who come in shepherd's clothing"?!

The shepherd feeds His flock.

The prophet told his people that God comes, rules, gathers, carries, leads, and feeds.

This passage of Isaiah reminds us of Luther's answer in the third article of the creed: "I believe that I cannot by my own understanding or effort believe in Jesus Christ my Lord, or come to him. But the Holy Spirit has called me through the Gospel, enlightened me with his gifts, and sanctified and kept me in true faith. In the same way he calls, gathers, enlightens, and sanctifies the whole Christian church on earth, and keeps it united with Jesus Christ in the one true faith...."

The shepherd Christ feeds His people. He promised the gift of the Holy Spirit. God is not dead. "Tell it on the mountain" as an anthem heralds and without fear announce that God is alive!

The earliest description in the Bible to call people to be missionaries is this call of the prophet. Other prophets had believed that Israel was to be a blessing to the families of the earth, but this prophet is the first to lay upon them the responsibility of heralding the gospel of their God. This is a turning point in the history of their nation. They are to be missionaries, evangelists.

Many among the exiles did not take the prophet at his word. However, some did. Cannot this be said of the Christian church? Christ's command is explicit in the great commission. The fear is not that people do not understand it. They understand it too well!

Lowell in his "Commemoration Ode" hailed the United States:

> " 'Tis no man we celebrate,...
> But the pith and marrow of a nation
> Drawing force from all her men...
> Pulsing it again through them,
> Till the basest can no longer cower,
> Touched but in passing by her mantle-hem."

The prophet thought of Jerusalem in the same way. The Christian is to think of the Christ that way. The "pith and marrow" of the Christian church is a loyal minority, in fellowship with God, carrying out His commands.

Christ has given us all the tools we need. He feeds us with the manger scene. He takes us on a hill not far away —not a mountain but a hill — a hill high enough for all people to see Him crucified. "For we do not proclaim ourselves; we proclaim Jesus Christ as Lord and ourselves as your slaves for Jesus' sake. For it is the God who said, 'Let light shine out of darkness' who has shone in our hearts to give the light of the knowledge of the glory of God in the face of Jesus Christ" (2 Corinthians 4:5-6).

The Christian knows Christ's face like the shepherd's face. This shepherd came to Bethlehem and rules hearts. The Christian knows that the real significance and impact of a person's life is determined by his priorities — those things he seeks above all else. One member said that due to the church and his work in charities, he had no time yet to buy Christmas presents for his family! That kind of priority in people the good shepherd brings out. Most of us want success and want to get ahead. What we want above all determines what kind of people we are to become. The kind of God you worship will determine your priorities and the kind of person you will be.

What is your God like? For the Christian, He is the God of two young boys in our family who pray each night:

Jesus, tender Shepherd, hear me
Bless thy little lambs tonight.
Through the darkness be thou near me,
Keep me safe till morning light.
Through this day Thy hand has led me,
And I thank thee for thy care;
Thou hast warmed me, clothed and fed me,
Listen to my evening prayer.
Let my sins be all forgiven;
Bless the friends I love so well;
Take me, Lord, at last to heaven,
Happy there with thee to dwell. Amen.

Is that your kind of God?

Sermon 24

What Christ Is Like —
An Angel

Text: Luke 2:10-12

"... the angel said to them, 'Do not be afraid; for see — I am bringing you good news of great joy for all the people: to you is born this day in the city of David a Savior, who is the Messiah, the Lord. This will be a sign for you: you will find a child wrapped in bands of cloth and lying in a manger."

This is the night of the angels. Shepherds were keeping their watch over their flock. Suddenly an angel appeared to them. There was more light around them than the huge lights that shine into the sky announcing a new Wal-Mart store!

Suppose you were walking through a field in the dark with only the bleating of sheep to keep you company. You would be afraid if suddenly a light blinded your eyes and a voice pierced the atmosphere. The shepherds were filled with fear.

These shepherds received a message that computers have not been able to emulate, "... be not afraid; for see — I am bringing you good news of great joy for all the people: to you is born this day in the city of David a Savior, who is the Messiah, the Lord."

An angel of the Lord brought this message. What would you answer if you were asked what an angel was? It is a difficult question.

You may have thought to yourself, when you heard young Donald sing tonight, "He sings like an angel." What do you mean? You have never heard an angel sing! When you and I make a statement like that we mean the singing was "heavenly." Why? Because we think of an angel coming from heaven. Christ is heavenly.

137

Christ came from heaven.

You and I may have differing views regarding angels. Whether you designate them as spiritual beings of a supernatural world or not will not necessarily brand your religion as valid or invalid. But what you think of Christ does determine the validity of your religion.

Many Americans are the victims of a religion known as "religious tolerance." Walter Barlow in his book *God so Loved* wrote, "It is only in the field of religion that we have come to exalt the mood of tolerance above all other intellectual virtues. ... Lacking a firsthand experience of Christ and His saving grace, multitudes of our church people are finding a spurious religious glow in movements that promise to bring the millennium by uniting all religious-minded people into one group by means of some magical formula which places fellowship above conviction" (p. 44).

Our schools omit God's teaching in their curriculum. What is left but atheism if God is eradicated from education? There seems to be one supreme loyalty, one conviction that shall rule — tolerance of everything. Some can only think of Christ as a teacher or a prophet. Some speak of Christ in the same tone of reverence when they speak of Abraham Lincoln. Some can teach we are only wayward children. All we need to know is the right direction to heaven!

One fundamentalist college advertised their campus was ten miles from any known sin. Someone exclaimed, "That would be a neat trick if you could do it!"

In the Incarnation, the birth of Christ, we see the confrontation of a sinful race with God's redeeming love. The angel's message of a Savior can be received only by those who believe we are by nature sinful and unclean, and need a Redeemer.

Christ came from heaven. It is this Divine initiative making possible the reconciliation with God. This Divine initiative lights up the fields of life. This Divine initiative destroys fear and replaces it with worship and obedience.

What do you think of this heavenly Christ? Christ said of himself: "Very truly, I tell you, before Abraham was, I am" (John 8:58). Christ claimed to exist from the beginning of time!

When Philip pleaded, "Lord, show us the Father, and we will be satisfied. Jesus said to him, 'Have I been with you all this time, Philip, and you still do not know me? Whoever has seen me has seen the Father' " (John 14:8-9).

What does Christ's visit to earth from heaven mean? We can say with Daniel T. Niles (*That They May Have Life*, p. 88):

> "Royalty hidden in a stable.
> Universality hidden in an exclusive race.
> True Divinity hidden in a man who experienced every
> human need and temptation.
> True Humanity hidden in a life of miracle — of spotless
> purity, stupendous authority and marvelous works.
> Voluntary self-giving hidden in a murder.
> Truth hidden in parables.
> The Resurrection hidden by its transcendence
> over common human experience.
> An eternal contemporaneousness."

Christ came from heaven to earth.

When you think of an angel, you think of Moses, David, the mother of Samson, Zechariah, or the shepherds at Bethlehem — someone standing beside you.

The great light that encircled the shepherds also encircled the angel. The angel speaks to the shepherds in their fields, not from some place in space. The angel's gentle encouragement "Be not afraid" stills their present terror. The same encouragement is given to us!

The dread of the unseen, which lies coiled like a sleeping snake in all hearts, is destroyed by the incarnation. God has entered history, so that the world might be reconciled to Him. Only God can stand by your side in the midst of fear and comfort you with His presence. Only God can stand by your side at the miracle of birth. Only God can stand by your side at grave's edge and say, "I am the resurrection and the life. Those who believe in me, even though they die, will live, and everyone who lives and believes in me, will never die. Do you believe this?" asked Jesus (John 11:25-26).

Like an angel, Christ comes by your side. A musician, when he was asked to compose a new national anthem for a European land, is reported to have said, "How can I? I wasn't born there." (Cited by George Buttrick, *Sermons Preached in a University Church*, p. 169.)

Christ was born here. He came to earth. He lived among us. "And the Word became flesh and lived among us..." (John 1:14). Christ is here now, in the midst of this congregation, among those who worship Him, among those who are gathered in His name.

God did not stop with the sending of a message with an angel; He came Himself! But the appearance of the angel to these humble men of the field symbolizes the destination of the gospel. The message was: "... I am bringing you good news of great joy for all the people: to you is born this day in the city of David a Savior, who is the Messiah, the Lord" (Luke 2:10-11).

It was not good news for Herod. It was an unhappy Christmas for him. He spent it by concocting a way of killing the Savior. He was afraid the Messiah would dethrone him. It was not good news for the high priest or the Pharisees and scribes. They spent harried days and nights trying to figure out how to trick and destroy the Messiah. It was not good news for Pilate. He had to make a decision that put his name in history books. It is good news for us. President Dwight Eisenhower said in these days of uncertainty "... the words of the angel have clearer understanding, sharper significance, more urgent counsel this Christmas."

It was good news for the shepherds. "Let us go now to Bethlehem and see this thing that has taken place, which the Lord has made known to us" (Luke 2:15). And they didn't waste any time getting there!

The great announcement, the mightiest, the most wonderful word that has ever passed angel's lips, is characterized as "... great joy for all the people..." (Luke 2:10). Nothing harmful can come out of the darkness from which Christ came. The significance of the incarnation is to envelop all believers!

Christ is King, not because of an accident of birth but because of who He is, Creator and Redeemer. He is priest, not because He ministered at an altar but because He Himself became the sacrifice. He is prophet not because of His teaching but because He is the Word of God.

Handel has gloriously given the spirit of the angel's news in the crash of the cymbal with which the last word peals out in his oratorio. "Savior" means much more than the shepherds knew at the moment. Savior means the deliverer from all evil, sin, and sorrow, and the endower of all that is good, of righteousness and blessedness. Christ is the fulfiller of prophecy, perfectly fulfilling His office as prophet, priest, and king. He is greater than Moses the law-giver; greater than Solomon in all his wisdom; greater than Jonah, the prophet. Christ is like an angel.

The similarity ends there. He is greater than an angel. Christ is God who came to earth. "Glory to God in the highest heaven, and on earth peace among those whom he favors" (Luke 2:14).

If this Savior God is what Christmas stripped of the tinsel and romance and myth is all about, we are in a quandary:

> "What tribute shall we pay
> To him who came in weakness,
> And in a manger lay
> To teach his people meekness?"

You have heard the legend of the shepherd maiden? When she watched the Magi place their rich gifts at the baby's feet, she was sad because she had no offering. She did not dare to enter the stable. She stood in the cold snow, and an angel saw her distress. The snow melted at her feet, perhaps from the warmth of her tears, and a small bush of winter roses grew in front of her as she watched. She took the roses, went inside, and worshiped the new-born King.

The important response of the wise men and the shepherds was they worshiped Him. The ultimate tribute is always ourselves, our very lives we offer to Him as "a reasonable, holy, and living sacrifice." No other tribute is enough.

This is the night of the angels. They come with the message "... of great joy for all the people...." So,

"Let ev'ry house be bright;
Let praises never cease.
With mercies infinite
Our Christ hath brought us peace."

Sermon 25

What Christ Is Like — A Master

Text: John 21:19b-24

> "Peter turned and saw the disciple whom Jesus loved following them; he was the one who had reclined at the supper and had said, 'Lord, who is it that is going to betray you?' When Peter saw him, he said to Jesus, 'Lord, what about him?'; Jesus said to him, 'If it is my will that he remain until I come, what is that to you? Follow me!' "
>
> — John 21:20-22

We have been studying some of the attributes and inherent qualities of our Lord and Savior during this Advent season. We have asked the question: What is your God like? We have said Christ is like a shepherd. He feeds His flock and tenderly cares for them. Christ is like an angel. God incarnate came to earth. His birth on this planet is the good news for all humanity. Worship the new-born King! Christ is like a child. Given a name that means "He will save His people from their sins," He was obedient throughout life and in death, even the death of the cross, and is the hope of the world.

In this sermon, last of the Christmas series, "What Christ Is Like — A Master," the scene swiftly changes from the manger to the Master after His resurrection.

The end of the year closes with the last words of John's gospel. It was this same gospel that began with the doctrinal statement, "In the beginning was the Word, and the Word was with God, and the Word was God" (John 1:1). Christ is that Word. He is the alpha and omega. John concludes, "But there are many other things that Jesus did; if every one of them were written down, I suppose that the world itself could not contain the books that would be written" (John 21:25).

143

We have stars here and there telling us of the constellations; a single star was enough to lead the wise men to Christ. That star shows us Christ as a Master. "The Master is come, and calleth for thee" (John 11:28, King James translation).

The church year beckons us to focus on Christ through John's eyes — apostle, evangelist. Peter said to Jesus, "Lord, what about him?" Jesus said, "If it is my will that he remain until I come, what is that to you? Follow me!"

Christ, like a Master, said, "If it is my will...."

Jesus spoke these words on the beach by the Sea of Tiberias. His resurrection proved He was the Master of death. This was the third time Jesus revealed Himself to the disciples.

After that early morning breakfast, Jesus took Peter aside and asked him, "Simon son of John, do you love me more than these?... Feed my lambs" (John 21:15). Peter was charged with a specific task. What made John bold enough to thrust himself into this interview? Peter saw him following. This was the same John, brother of James, son of Zebedee, who was a Galilean fisherman. John was one of the earliest disciples called to follow Christ. John and his brother, James, had asked special honors for themselves and yet declared they were ready to face death with Christ. Jesus called them "Boanerges" — "sons of thunder." But John was known as "the disciple whom Jesus loved" (John 21:20). At the cross, John alone was faithful and was entrusted with the care of Jesus' mother. At the tomb, John was the first to believe in Jesus' resurrection. At the Sea of Galilee, John first recognized Christ. Peter wanted to know about John. What was his task to be? "Lord, what about him?" Jesus said to Peter, "If it is my will that he remain until I come, what is that to you? Follow me!"

The Master is speaking and has the right to direct His servants. He has the right to assign work to His believers. "Indeed, just as the Father raises the dead and gives them life, so also the Son gives life to whomever he wishes" (John 5:21). Paul wrote in Romans 13:9, "For to this end Christ died and lived again, so that he might be Lord of both the dead and the living."

These two apostles, Peter and John, became full proof of Christ's claim, Master of all. Peter was imprisoned and delivered once. The second imprisonment of Peter ended with his martyrdom, not because of his prosecutors' strength but the will of the Master.

John was assigned a longer life. No doubt there were times when he longed to depart this earthly life. He saw his brother James slain, the first of the apostles to be killed. This same brother and Peter had been very close to our Lord – at the raising of Jairus' daughter (Mark 5:37; Luke 5:51), at the Transfiguration (Matthew 17:1; Mark 9:2; Luke 9:28), and at Gethsemane (Matthew 26:37; Mark 14:33). No doubt John would have welcomed martyrdom. To him to live was martyrdom. He had to wait until the Master came and called him.

John saw Jesus as the Master of life and death. The hands that were nailed to the cross were the same hands that turned the key of death. Anyone who believes in this Master entrusts life to Him and bows his will to Him.

Like a Master, Jesus said....

"If it is my will that he remain until I come, what is that to you? Follow me!"

The roles of Peter and John were to be different. Peter was a man of action, full of impulse, restless until his hands could do something to express his thoughts and actions. On the Mount of Transfiguration he wanted to work and build something. In Galilee he could not sit and do nothing. He told his friends, "I am going fishing" (John 21:3). When Peter saw Jesus on the shore he could not wait for the boat to land, so he dove into the water and swam to shore. Throughout the book of Acts there are episodes of Peter's dynamic preaching and ministry, healing the sick or confronting the Sanhedrin. Peter's role was one of action, in the shock of conflict and in the strain of work.

John's role is different from Peter's. You don't hear much about his work in the writings. He stands as the silent figure by the side of Peter. We do not hear of his works. John is to "... remain until I come." He is to tarry and abide. Evidently his brethren misinterpreted what Jesus said. They thought of John as another Enoch. John himself corrects this in his gospel. "So the rumor spread in the community that this disciple would not die. Yet Jesus did not say to him that he would not die, but 'If it is my will that he remain until I come, what is that to you?' " (John 21:23).

John is the quiet type. His life is one of contemplation which bore fruit. The epistles of John and the book of Revelation, in addition to the fourth gospel, are attributed to him. The "son of thunder" mellowed under the Master's influence.

The Master had work for Peter and John. But the work was to be different. Jesus did not try to cast every person into the same mold. In an age when the "Organization Man" is the norm, it is good for us to recognize the danger of pure activity. The strain of our everyday life, our feverish desire for immediate results, assumes Christianity is nothing if not practical.

A man exclaimed to me, "Pastor, show me your Christianity works and I will believe it and change my ways." I answered, "My friend, Christianity is not a 'do it yourself religion.' It isn't something that you build, not even the kingdom, and say 'there it is' and step back and admire it." "God's kingdom comes indeed without our praying for it, but we ask in this prayer that it may come also to us." (Luther's answer in the second petition of The Lord's Prayer.)

The good and the bad in Christians is this: If people are not in some external work in a life of Christian service for the good of others, we judge them to be inactive. Too many people do nothing in the Christian church. It is true also that quiet contemplation, communion with God is necessary before anything lasting occurs. The stream that was to water a community began as a trickle high in the mountain!

A Martha always thinks Mary is idle by sitting at Jesus' feet. There are people who cannot work much. There are also people who can't think much. We all need to listen to the Master, "Come away to a deserted place all by yourselves and rest a while" (Mark 6:31).

Work is good. But the foundation of work is better. Activity is good. But the foundation, the basis of the activity, is better. Let Peter fan the flame, confront the high priests, and stir the fight. Let John write, care for Jesus' mother, and bring us closer to Christ with His great sense of love.

Like a Master, Christ does not always let us know what His will is.

The disciples did not know what Jesus meant when He referred to John as the remaining disciple. It is quite likely that at the time John did not know what Jesus meant since these words of John were recorded last. But in patient acquiescence, John learned the meaning of Christ's will.

Is it important to know the future? It always grieves me to hear of Christians going to fortune tellers, even if they go only in fun. I have seen predictions of fortune tellers change lives and not always for the best. Life is not made up of wishful thinking. Your life is designed by God. Only He can change your life.

What a wonderful life for believers, that in quiet submission, not indifference, we abide in God's word and live in the undisclosed will of our loving Christ.

I don't know what your future holds. I don't even know the church's future. I do know that belief in Christ is sufficient. The alternatives of life and death loom large for those who do not know Christ. For Christians, it does not matter. There will be work for us to do and the love of a Master Lord to possess us if we live throughout the new year. If we die sometime in the coming year, there will be work for us to do then, and a love to possess us in still more abundant measure.

Are you ready to let the coming year be in God's hands? Do the fears and anxieties, even death itself, mean little to you? Can you say these things will not touch your truest self? Are you able, are you content to leave all uncertainty to God. Will you be content with His decisions? Are you content with uncertainty, leaving it all to God? This does not mean that we do nothing. It does mean we live with God's directions instead of our decisions. Are you willing to follow God's directions?

Your answers will tell you what you think of Christ. What does Jesus mean to you? Is Christ like a shepherd? Is Christ like an angel? Is Christ like a child? Is Christ like a Master?

In the final analysis: Have you entrusted your sinful soul for salvation to Jesus Christ? If you have, then it will not matter what happens to you in the coming year or what your future might be.